Explorers book
from
S W Cong
1926
1919

BULGARIA

Uniform with this Volume

AUSTRIA-HUNGARY
ENGLAND
FRANCE
ITALY
SWITZERLAND

A. AND C. BLACK, LTD.,
4 SOHO SQUARE, LONDON, W.

A YOUNG SHÔP MAN OF THE DISTRICT OF SOFIA

Frontispiece

BULGARIA

BY

FRANK FOX

AUTHOR OF "ENGLAND," "ITALY," AND
"SWITZERLAND"

WITH 32 FULL-PAGE ILLUSTRATIONS IN COLOUR

LONDON
A. AND C. BLACK, LIMITED
1915

CONTENTS

CHAPTER I
By Way of Introduction 1

CHAPTER II
Bulgaria and the Death of the Roman Empire . 15

CHAPTER III
The Scrap-Heap of Races 36

CHAPTER IV
Bulgaria—A Power and a Turkish Province . . 52

CHAPTER V
The Liberation of Bulgaria 65

CHAPTER VI
The War of 1912–1913 77

CHAPTER VII

A War Correspondent's Trials in Bulgaria . . 99

CHAPTER VIII

Incidents of Bulgarian Character 120

CHAPTER IX

The Tragedy of 1914 134

CHAPTER X

Some Facts for the Tourist and the Economist . 150

CHAPTER XI

How Bulgaria is Governed 167

CHAPTER XII

The Future of Bulgaria 174

CHAPTER XIII

The Responsibility of Europe 187

INDEX 207

LIST OF ILLUSTRATIONS

By JAN V. MRKVITCHKA and NOEL POCOCK*

1.	A Young Shôp Man of the District of Sofia	*Frontispiece*
		FACING PAGE
2.	A Contented Turk	8
3.	A Peasant at Work—District of Tsaribrod . .	17
4.	Women of Pordim, in the Plevna District . .	19
5.	In the Harvest Fields near Sofia . . .	22
6.	A Shôp Woman of the District of Sofia . . .	24
7.	A Woman of Thrace, of the Shôp Tribe, and of Macedonia	33
8.	*Sistov, on the Danube	40
9.	Ancient Costume of Balkan Peasant Women near Gabrovo	49
10.	A Wedding in the Rhodopes	56
11.	*Roustchouk, on the Danube	65
12.	" Mystery "—a Study in the Roustchouk District .	67
13.	A Blind Beggar Woman	70
14.	A Young Married Shôp Woman	72
15.	*A Bulgarian Market Town	75
16.	Blessing the Lamb on St. George's Day . . .	78

BULGARIA

		FACING PAGE
17.	*The Cathedral, Sofia	81
18.	*An Adrianople Street	88
19.	*The Shipka Pass	97
20.	A Young Widow at her Husband's Grave . .	104
21.	Gipsies	113
22.	A Peasant of the Tsaribrod District	120
23.	The Ratchenitza, the National Dance of Bulgaria .	129
24.	A Bagpiper	136
25.	A Young Girl of Irn	145
26.	Guarding the Flocks and Herds	152
27.	An Old Street in Philippopolis	161
28.	A Grave Question	168
29.	A Young Man of the Choumla District . . .	177
30.	*A Bulgarian Farm	184
31.	A Young Woman of the Roustchouk District . .	193
32.	At the Well	200

Sketch Map at end of Volume.

BULGARIA

CHAPTER I

BY WAY OF INTRODUCTION

INSTRUCTED in the autumn of 1912 to join the Bulgarian army, then mobilising for war against Turkey, as war correspondent for the *London Morning Post*, I made my preparations with the thought uppermost that I was going to a cut-throat country where massacre was the national sport and human life was regarded with no sentimental degree of respect. The Bulgarians, a generation ago, had been paraded before the eyes of the British people by the fiery eloquence of Mr. Gladstone as a deeply suffering people, wretched victims of Turkish atrocities. After the wide sympathy that followed his Bulgarian Atrocities campaign there came a strong reaction. It was maintained that the Bulgarians were by no means the blameless victims of the Turks; and could themselves initiate massacres as well as suffer from them. Some even charged that there was a good deal of party spirit to account for the heat of Mr. Gladstone's championship. I think that the average British opinion in 1912 was that, regarding the quarrels between Bulgar and Turk, there was a great deal to be said against both sides; and that no Balkan people was worth a moment's sentimental worry. "Let dogs delight to bark and bite, for 'tis their nature to," expressed the common view when one heard that there had been murders and village-burnings again in the Balkans.

Certainly there were enthusiasts who held to the old Gladstonian faith that there was some peculiar merit in the Bulgarian people which justified all that they did, and which would justify Great Britain in going into the most dangerous of wars on their behalf. These enthusiasts, as if to make more startlingly clear their love for Bulgaria, commonly took a profoundly pacific view of all other questions of international politics, and would become passionately indignant at the suggestion that the British Power should ever move navy or army in defence of any selfish

British interest. They were—they still are, it may be said—the leading lights of what is called the Peace-at-any-price party, detesting war and "jingoism," and viewing patriotism, when found growing on British soil, with dry suspicion. Patriotism in Bulgaria is, however, to their view a growth of a different order, worthy to be encouraged and sheltered at any cost.

As a counter-weight to these enthusiasts, Great Britain sheltered a little band, usually known as pro-Turks, who believed, with almost as passionate a sincerity as that of the pro-Bulgarians, that the Turk was the only gentleman in Europe, and that his mild and blameless aspirations towards setting up the perfect State were being cruelly thwarted by the abominable Bulgars and other Balkan riff-raff. Good government in the Balkans would come, they held, if the tide of Turkish rule flowed forward and the restless, semi-savage, murderous Balkan Christian states went back to peace and philosophic calm under the wise rule of Cadi administering the will of the Khalifate.

But pro-Bulgarian and pro-Turk made comparatively few converts in Great Britain. They formed influential little groups and inspired debates in the House of Lords and the House of Commons, and published literature, and went out as missions to their beloved nationalities, and had all their affection confirmed again by the fine appreciation showered upon them. The great mass of British public opinion, however, they did not touch. There was never a second flaming campaign because of Turkish atrocities towards Bulgaria, and the pro-Turks never had a sufficient sense of humour to suggest a counter-campaign when Bulgarians made reprisals. In official circles the general attitude towards Balkan affairs was one of vexation alternating with indifference.

"Those detestable Balkans!" quoth one diplomat in an undiplomatic moment: and expressed well the official mind. "They are six of one and half a dozen of the other," said the man in the street when he heard of massacres, village-burnings, and tortures in the Balkans; and he turned to the football news with undisturbed mind, seeking something on which a fair opinion could be formed without too much worry.

The view of the man in the street was my view in 1912. I can recall being contented in my mind

BY WAY OF INTRODUCTION 5

to know that at any rate one's work as a war correspondent would not be disturbed by any sympathy for the one side or the other. Whichever side lost it would deserve to have lost, and whatever reduction in the population of the Balkan Peninsula was caused by the war would be ultimately a benefit to Europe. In parts of America where the race feeling is strongest, they say that the only good nigger is a dead nigger. So I felt about the Balkan populations. The feelings of a man with some interest in flocks of sheep on hearing that war had broken out between the wolves and the jackals would represent fairly well the attitude of mind in which I packed my kit for the Balkans.

It is well to put on record that mental foundation on which I built up my impressions of the Balkans generally, and of the Bulgarian people particularly, for at the present time (1914) I think it may safely be said that the Bulgarian people are somewhat under a cloud, and are not standing too high in the opinion of the civilised world. Yet, to give an honest record of my observations of them, I shall have to praise them very highly in some respects. Whilst it would be going too far to say that the praise is reluctant, it is true that it has been in a way forced from me, for I went to Bulgaria with the prejudice against the Bulgarians that I have indicated. And—to make this explanation complete—I may add that I came back from the Balkans not a pro-Bulgarian in the sense that I was anti-Greek or anti-Servian or even anti-Turk; but with a feeling of general liking for all the peasant peoples whom a cruel fate has cast into the Balkans to fight out there national and racial issues, some of which are older than the Christian era.

Yes, even the Turk, the much-maligned Turk, proved to have decent possibilities if given a decent chance. Certainly he is no longer the Terrible Turk of tradition. Most of the Turks I encountered in Bulgaria were prisoners of war, evidently rather pleased to be in the hands of the Bulgarians who fed them decently, a task which their own commissariat had failed in: or were contented followers of menial occupations in Bulgarian towns. I can recall Turkish boot-blacks and Turkish porters, but no Turks who looked like warriors, and if they are cut-throats by choice (I do not believe they are) they are very mild-mannered cut-throats indeed.

Coming back from the lines of Chatalja towards

A CONTENTED TURK

BY WAY OF INTRODUCTION 7

the end of 1912, I had, for one stage of five days, between Kirk Kilisse and Mustapha Pasha, a Turkish driver. He had been a Bulgarian subject (I gathered) before the war, and with his cart and two horses had been impressed into the transport service. At first with some aid from an interpreter, afterwards mostly by signs and broken fragments of language, I got to be able to converse with this Turk. (In the Balkans the various shreds of races have quaint crazy-quilt patchworks of conversational language. Somehow or other even a British citizen with more than the usual stupidity of our race as to foreign languages can make himself understood in the Balkan Peninsula, which is so polyglottic that its inhabitants understand signs very well.) My Turk friend, from the very first, filled my heart with sympathy because of his love for his horses. Since he had come under the war-rule of the Bulgarians, he complained to me, he had not been allowed to feed his horses properly. They were fading away. He wept over them. Actual tears irrigated the furrows of his weather-beaten and unwashed cheeks.

As a matter of fact the horses were in very good condition indeed, considering all the circumstances; as good, certainly, as any horses I had seen since I left Buda-Pesth. But my heart warmed to this Turcoman and his love for his horses. I had been seeking in vain up to this point for the appearance of the Terrible Turk of tradition; the Turk, with his well-beloved Arabian steed, his quite-secondary-in-consideration Circassian harem; the fierce, unconquerable, disdainful, cruel Turk, manly in his vices as well as in his virtues. My Turk had at least one recognisable characteristic in his love for his horses. As he sorrowed over them I comforted him with a flagon—it was of brandy and water : and the Prophet, when he forbade wine, was ignorant of brandy, so Islam these days has its alcoholic consolation—and I stayed him with cigarettes. He had not had a smoke for a month and, put in possession of tobacco, he plunged into a mood of rapt exultation, rolling cigarette after cigarette, chuckling softly as he inhaled the smoke, turning towards me now and again with a gesture of thanks and of respect. I had taken over the reins and the little horses were doing very well.

That day, though we had started late, the horses carried us thirty-five miles, and I camped at the site of a burned-out village. The Turk made no objection to this. Previously coming over the same route with an ox-cart, my Macedonian driver had objected to camping except in occupied villages where there were garrisons. He feared Bashi-Bazouks (the Turkish irregular bands which occasionally showed themselves in the rear of the Bulgarian army) and wolves. Probably, too, he feared ghosts, or was uneasy and lonely when out of range of the village smells. Now I preferred a burned village site, because the only clean villages were the burned ones; and for the reason of water it was necessary to camp at some village or village site. Mr. Turk went up hugely in my estimation when I found that he had no objections to the site of a burned village as a camping-place.

But the first night in camp shattered all my illusions. The Turk unharnessed and lit the camp fire. I cooked my supper and gave him a share. Then he squatted by the fire and resumed smoking. The horses over which he had shed tears waited. After the Turk's third cigarette I suggested that the horses should be watered and fed. The village well was about 300 yards away, and the Turk evidently did not like the idea of moving from the fire. He did not move, but argued in Turkish of which I understood nothing. Finally I elicited the fact that the horses were too tired to drink and too tired to eat the barley I had brought for them. As a remedy for tiredness they were to be left without water and food all night.

As plainly as was possible I insisted to the Turk that the horses must be watered at once, and afterwards given a good ration of barley. I dragged him from the fire to the horses and made my meaning clear enough. The Turk was stubborn. Clearly either I was to water the horses myself or they were to be left without water, and my old traditions of horse-mastery would not allow me to have them fed without being watered. So this was the extent of the Turk's devotion to his horses!

It was necessary to be firm, and I took up the cart whip to the Turk and convinced him almost at once that the horses were not " too tired " to drink.

Mr. Turk did not resent the blows in the least. He refrained from cutting my throat as I slept that evening. Afterwards a mere wave of the hand towards the whip made him move with alacrity. At the end of the journey, when I gave him a good "tip," he knelt down gallantly in the mud of Mustapha Pasha and kissed my hand and carried it to his forehead.

So faded away my last hope of meeting the Terrible Turk of tradition in the Balkans. Perhaps he exists still in Asia Minor. As I saw the Turk in Bulgaria and in European Turkey, he was a dull monogamic person with no fiery pride, no picturesque devilry, but a great passion for sweetmeats—not merely his own "Turkish Delight," but all kinds of lollipops : his shops were full of Scotch and English confectionery.

But the Bulgarian, not the Turk, is our theme. This introduction, however, will make it plain that, as the result of a direct knowledge of the Balkans, during some months in which I had the opportunity of sharing in Bulgarian peasant life, I came to the admiration I have now for the Bulgarian people in spite of a preliminary prejudice. And this conversion of view was not the result of becoming involved in some passionate political attitude regarding Balkan affairs. I am not now prepared to take up the view of the fanatic Bulgar-worshippers who must not only exalt the Bulgarian nation as a modern Chosen

People, but must represent Servian, Greek, and Turk as malignant and devilish in order to throw up in the highest light their ideas of Bulgarian saintliness.

The Balkans are apt to have strange effects on the traveller. Perhaps it is the blood-mist that hangs always over the Balkan plains and glens which gets into the head and intoxicates one: perhaps it is the call to the wild in us from the primitive human nature of the Balkan peoples. Whatever the reason, it is a common thing for the unemotional English traveller to go to the Balkans as a tourist and return as a passionate enthusiast for some Balkan Peninsula nationality. He becomes, perhaps, a pro-Turk, and thereafter will argue with fierceness that the Turk is the only man who leads an idyllic life in Europe to-day, and that the way to human regeneration is through a conversion to Turkishness. He fills his house with Turkish visitors and writes letters to the papers pointing out the savagery we show in the "Turk's Head" competition for our cavalry-men at military tournaments. Or he may become a pro-Bulgar with a taste for the company of highly flavoured Macedonian revolutionary priests and a grisly habit of turning

BY WAY OF INTRODUCTION 13

the conversation to the subject of outrage and massacre. To become a pro-Servian is not a common fashion, but pro-Albanians and pro-Montenegrins and Philhellenists are common enough.

The word "crank," if it can be read in a kindly sense and stripped of malice, covers all these folk. Exactly why the Balkans have such an effect in making "cranks" I have already confessed an inability to explain. The fact must stand as one of those things which we must believe—if we read Parliamentary debates and newspaper correspondence—but cannot comprehend.

But any "crank" view I disavow. Whether from a natural lack of a generous sense of partisanship, or a journalistic training (which crabs emotionalism: that acute observer of men, the late "General" Booth, said once of his Salvation Army work, "You can never 'save' a journalist"), I came back from the Balkans without a desire to join a society to exalt any one of the little nationalities struggling for national expression in its rowdy life. But I did get to a strong admiration of the Bulgarian people as soldiers, farmers, road-makers, and as friends. The evidence on which that admiration is based will be stated in these pages, and it is my hope that it will do a little to set the Bulgarian—who is sometimes much overpraised and often much over-abused—in a right light before my readers.

But before dealing with the Bulgarian of to-day we must look into his antecedents.

CHAPTER II

BULGARIA AND THE DEATH OF THE ROMAN EMPIRE

PROBABLY not the least part of the interest which the traveller or the student will take in Bulgaria is the fact that it was the arena in which were fought the great battles of races declaring the doom of the Roman Empire. Fortunately, from old Gothic chronicles it is possible to get pictures —valuable for vivid colouring rather than strict accuracy—which bring very close to us that curious tragedy of civilisation, the destruction of the power of Rome and the overrunning of Europe by successive waves of barbarians.

In the fifth century before Christ, what is now Bulgaria was practically a Greek colony, and its trading relations with the North gave possibly the first hint to the Goths of the easiest path by which to invade the Roman Empire. The present Bulgarian towns of Varna (on the Black Sea) and Kustendji (which has a literary history in that it was later a place of banishment for Ovid the poet) can be traced back as Greek trading towns through which passed traffic from the Mediterranean to the " Scythians," *i.e.* the Goths of the North. Amber and furs came from the north of the river valleys, and caravans from the south brought in return silver and gold and bronze.

Towards the dawn of the Christian era there began a swelling-over of the Goths from the Baltic shores, sending one wave of invasion down towards Italy, another towards the Black Sea and the Aegean. Jordanes, the earliest Gothic historian, writing in the sixth century gives this account—derived from Gothic folk-songs—of the movement of the invasion towards the Balkan Peninsula (probably about A.D. 170):

In the reign of the fifth King after Berig, Filimer, son of Gadariges, the people had so greatly increased in numbers that they all agreed in the conclusion that the army of the Goths should move forward with their families in quest of more fitting abodes. Thus they came to those regions of Scythia which in their tongue are called Oium, whose great fertility pleased them much. But there was a bridge there by which the army

A PEASANT AT WORK, DISTRICT OF TSARIBROD

essayed to cross a river, and when half of the army had passed, that bridge fell down in irreparable ruin, nor could any one either go forward or return. For that place is said to be girt round with a whirlpool, shut in with quivering morasses, and thus by her confusion of the two elements, land and water, Nature has rendered it inaccessible. But in truth, even to this day, if you may trust the evidence of passers-by, though they go not nigh the place, the far-off voices of cattle may be heard and traces of men may be discerned.

That part of the Goths therefore which under the leadership of Filimer crossed the river and reached the lands of Oium, obtained the longed-for soil. Then without delay they came to the nation of the Spali, with whom they engaged in battle and therein gained the victory. Thence they came forth as conquerors, and hastened to the farthest part of Scythia which borders on the Black Sea.

The people whom these Teutonic Goths displaced were Slavs. The Goths settled down first on the Black Sea between the mouths of the Danube and of the Dniester and beyond that river almost to the Don, becoming thus neighbours of the Huns on the east, of the Roman Empire's Balkan colonies on the west, and of the Slavs on the north. It is reasonable to suppose that to some extent they mingled their blood somewhat with the Slavs whom they dispossessed, and that they came into some contact with the Huns also.

It was in the third century of the Christian era that these Goths, who had been for some time subsidised by the Roman emperors on the condition that they kept the peace, crossed the Danube and devastated Moesia and Thrace. An incident of this invasion was the successful resistance of the garrison of Marcianople—now Schumla—to the invaders. In a following campaign the Goths crossed the Danube at Novae (now Novo-grad) and besieged Philippopolis, a city which still keeps its name and now, as then, is an important strategical point commanding the Thracian Plain. (It was Philippopolis which would have been the objective of the Turkish attack upon Bulgaria in 1912–13 if Turkey had been given a chance in that war to develop a forward movement.) This city was taken by the Goths, and the first notable Balkan massacre is recorded, over 100,000 people being put to the sword within its walls. Later in the campaign the Emperor Decius was defeated and killed by the Goths in a battle waged on marshy ground near the mouth of the Danube. This was the second of the three great disasters which marked the doom of the Roman Empire: the first was the defeat of Varus in Germany; the third was

WOMEN OF PORDIM, IN THE PLEVNA DISTRICT

to be the defeat and death of the Emperor Valens before Adrianople. Bulgaria, the scene of the second and third disasters, can accurately be described as having provided the death-arena for Rome.

From the defeat of Decius (A.D. 251) may be said to date the Gothic colonisation of the Balkan Peninsula. True, after that event the Goths often retired behind the Danube for a time, but, as a rule, thereafter they were steadily encroaching on the Roman territory, carrying on a maritime war in the Black Sea as well as land forays across the Danube. It was because of the successes of the Goths in the Balkans that the decision was ultimately arrived at to move the capital of the Roman Empire from Rome to Constantinople. During the first Gothic attack, after the death of Decius, Byzantium itself was threatened, and the cities around the Sea of Marmora sacked. An incident of this invasion which has been chronicled is that the Goths enjoyed hugely the warm baths they found at Anchialus—" there were certain warm springs renowned above all others in the world for their healing virtues, and greatly did the Goths delight to wash therein. And having tarried there many days they thence returned home." Now Anchialus is clearly identifiable as the present Bulgarian town of Bourgas, a flourishing seaport connected by rail with Jambouli and still noted for its baths.

In a later Gothic campaign (A.D. 262), based on a naval expedition from the Black Sea, Byzantium was taken, the Temple of Diana at Ephesus destroyed, and Athens sacked. A German historian pictures this last incident:

> The streets and squares which at other times were enlivened only by the noisy crowds of the ever-restless citizens, and of the students who flocked thither from all parts of the Graeco-Roman world, now resounded with the dull roar of the German bull-horns and the war-cry of the Goths. Instead of the red cloak of the Sophists, and the dark hoods of the Philosophers, the skin-coats of the barbarians fluttered in the breeze. Wodan and Donar had gotten the victory over Zeus and Athene.

It was in regard to this capture of Athens that the story was first told—it has been told of half a dozen different sackings since—that a band of Goths came upon a library and were making a bonfire of its contents when one of their leaders interposed:

> "Not so, my sons; leave these scrolls untouched, that the Greeks may in time to come, as they have in time

past, waste their manhood in poring over their wearisome contents. So will they ever fall, as now, an easy prey to the strong unlearned sons of the North."

In the ultimate result the Goths were driven out of Athens by a small force led by Dexippus, a soldier and a scholar whose exploit revived memory of the deeds of Greece in her greatness. The capture of Athens deeply stirred the civilised world of the day, and " Goth " still survives as a term of destructive barbarism.

A few years later (A.D. 269) the Goths began a systematic invasion of the Balkan provinces of the Roman Empire, attacking the Roman territory both by sea and by land. The tide of victory sometimes turned for a while, and at Naissus (now Nish in Servia, near the border of Bulgaria) the Goths were defeated by the Emperor Claudius. Their defeated army was then shut up in the Balkan Mountains for a winter, and the Gothic power in the Balkans temporarily crushed. The Emperor Claudius, who took the surname Gothicus in celebration of his victory, announced it grandiloquently to the governor of Illyricum :

Claudius to Brocchus.

We have destroyed 320,000 of the Goths ; we have sunk 2000 of their ships. The rivers are bridged over with shields; with swords and lances all the shores are covered. The fields are hidden from sight under the superincumbent bones; no road is free from them; an immense encampment of waggons is deserted. We have taken such a number of women that each soldier can have two or three concubines allotted to him.

But the succeeding Emperor, Aurelian, gave up all Dacia to the Goths and withdrew the Romanised Dacians into the province of Moesia—made up of what is now Eastern Servia and Western Bulgaria. This province was divided into two and renamed Dacia. One part, Dacia Mediterranea, had for its capital Sardica, now Sofia, the capital of Bulgaria. Then followed a period of comparative peace. The Roman emperors saw that on the Balkan frontier their Empire had to be won or lost, and strengthened the defences there. Thus Diocletian made his headquarters at Nicomedia. Finally, Constantine moved the capital altogether to Constantinople. Goth and Roman at this time showed a disposition to a peaceful amalgamation, and the Bulgarian population was rapidly becoming a Romano-Gothic one. Christianity had been introduced, and the Gothic historian Jordanes tells of a Gothic people living upon the northern side of the Balkan Mountains:

IN THE HARVEST-FIELDS NEAR SOFIA

There were also certain other Goths, who are called Minores, an immense people, with their bishop and primate Vulfila, who is said, moreover, to have taught them letters; and they are at this day dwelling in Moesia, in the district called Nicopolitana [1] at the foot of Mount Haemus, a numerous race, but poor and unwarlike, abounding only in cattle of divers kinds, and rich in pastures and forest timber, having little wheat, though the earth is fertile in producing other crops. They do not appear to have any vineyards: those who want wine buy it of their neighbours; but most of them drink only milk.

A contemporary of the saintly Ulfilas (who surely should be accepted as the first national hero of the Bulgarians) states that Ulfilas had originally lived on the other side of the Danube and had been driven by persecution to settle in Bulgaria. This contemporary, Auxentius, records:

And when, through the envy and mighty working of the enemy, there was kindled a persecution of the Christians by an irreligious and sacrilegious Judge of the Goths, who spread tyrannous affright through the barbarian land, it came to pass that Satan, who desired to do evil, unwillingly did good; that those whom he sought to make deserters became confessors of the faith; that the persecutor was conquered, and his victims wore the wreath of victory. Then, after the glorious martyrdom of many servants and handmaids of Christ, as the

---

[1] Around the modern town of Tirnova.

persecution still raged vehemently, after seven years of his episcopate were expired, the blessed Ulfilas being driven from " Varbaricum " with a great multitude of confessors, was honourably received on the soil of Roumania by the Emperor Constantius of blessed memory. Thus as God by the hand of Moses delivered His people from the violence of Pharaoh and the Egyptians, and made them pass through the Red Sea, and ordained that they should serve Him [on Mount Sinai], even so by means of Ulfilas did God deliver the confessors of His only-begotten Son from the " Varbarian " land, and cause them to cross over the Danube, and serve Him upon the mountains [of Haemus] like his saints of old.

Ulfilas civilised as well as Christianised the Goths of Bulgaria, and was responsible for the earliest Gothic alphabet—the Moeso-Gothic. He translated most of the Scriptures into Gothic, leaving out of his translation only such war stories as " the Book of Kings," judging that these would be too exciting for his Gothic flock and would incite them to war.

After a century of peace war broke out again between the Goths and the Roman Empire—which may now be called rather the Greek Empire—in A.D. 369. The course of the war was at first favourable to the Emperor Valens. All the independent Goths were driven back behind the Danube boundary, but were allowed to live there

A SHÔP WOMAN OF THE DISTRICT OF SOFIA

in peace. The Roman orator Themistius, in congratulating the Emperor Valens, put on record the extent of his achievement and of his magnanimity:

But now, along almost all the frontiers of the Empire, peace reigns, and all the preparation for war is perfect; for the Emperor knows that they most truly work for peace who thoroughly prepare for war. The Danube-shore teems with fortresses, the fortresses with soldiers, the soldiers with arms, the arms both beautiful and terrible. Luxury is banished from the legions, but there is an abundance of all necessary stores, so that there is now no need for the soldier to eke out his deficient rations by raids on the peaceful villagers. There was a time when the legions were terrible to the provincials, and afraid of the barbarians. Now all that is changed: they despise the barbarians and fear the complaint of one plundered husbandman more than an innumerable multitude of Goths.

To conclude, then, as I began. We celebrate this victory by numbering not our slaughtered foes but our living and tamed antagonists. If we regret to hear of the entire destruction even of any kind of animal, if we mourn that elephants should be disappearing from the province of Africa, lions from Thessaly, and hippopotami from the marshes of the Nile, how much rather, when a whole nation of men, barbarians it is true, but still men, lies prostrate at our feet, confessing that it is entirely at our mercy, ought we not instead of extirpating, to preserve it, and make it our own by showing it compassion?

Valens restored Bulgaria to the position of a wholly Roman province, even the Gothic Minores being driven across the Danube. But there was now to come another racial element into the making of Bulgaria—the Huns.

I can still recall the resentment and indignation of the Bulgarian officers in 1913 because a French war correspondent had, in a despatch which had escaped the Censor, likened the crossing of the Thracian Plain by the great convoys of Bulgarian ox-wagons to the passage of the Danube by the Huns in the fourth century. The Bulgarians, always inclined to be sensitive, thought that the allusion made them out to be barbarians. But it was intended rather, I think, to show the writer's knowledge of the early history of the Balkan Peninsula and of the close racial ties between the Bulgarians of to-day and the original Huns. We have seen how the Gothic invasion, coming from the Baltic to the Black Sea, pushed on to the borders of the Hun people living east of the Volga. These Huns now prepared an answering wave of invasion.

To the Goths the Huns—the first of the Tartar hordes to invade Europe—were a source of superstitious terror. The Gothic historian Jordanes writes with frank horror of them:

We have ascertained that the nation of the Huns, who surpassed all others in atrocity, came thus into being. When Filimer, fifth king of the Goths, after their departure from Sweden, was entering Scythia, with his people, as we have before described, he found among them certain sorcerer-women, whom they call in their native tongue Haliorunnas, whom he suspected and drove forth from his army into the wilderness. The unclean spirits that wander up and down in desert places, seeing these women, made concubines of them; and from this union sprang that most fierce people, the Huns, who were at first little, foul, emaciated creatures, dwelling among the swamps and possessing only the shadow of human speech by way of language.

According to Priscus they settled first on the eastern shore of the Sea of Azof, lived by hunting, and increased their substance by no kind of labour, but only by defrauding and plundering their neighbours.

Once upon a time when they were out hunting beside the Sea of Azof, a hind suddenly appeared before them, and having entered the water of that shallow sea, now stopping, now dashing forward, seemed to invite the hunters to follow on foot. They did so, through what they had before supposed to be trackless sea with no land beyond it, till at length the shore of Scythia lay before them. As soon as they set foot upon it, the stag that had guided them thus far mysteriously disappeared. This, I trow, was done by those evil spirits that begat them, for the injury of the Goths. But the hunters who had lived in complete ignorance of any other land beyond the Sea of Azof were struck with admiration of the Scythian land and deemed that a path known to no previous age had been divinely revealed to them. They returned to their comrades to tell them what had happened, and the whole nation resolved to follow the track thus opened out before them. They crossed that vast pool, they fell like a human whirlwind on the nations inhabiting that part of Scythia, and offering up the first tribes whom they overcame, as a sacrifice to victory, suffered the others to remain alive, but in servitude.

With the Alani especially, who were as good warriors as themselves, but somewhat less brutal in appearance and manner of life, they had many a struggle, but at length they wearied out and subdued them. For, in truth, they derived an unfair advantage from the intense hideousness of their countenances. Nations whom they would never have vanquished in fair fight fled horrified from those frightful—faces I can hardly call them, but rather—shapeless black collops of flesh, with little points instead of eyes. No hair on their cheeks or chins gives grace to adolescence or dignity to age, but deep furrowed scars instead, down the sides of their faces, show the impress of the iron which with characteristic ferocity they apply to every male child that is born among them, drawing blood from its cheeks before it is allowed its first taste of milk. They are little in stature, but lithe and active in their motions, and especially skilful in riding, broad-shouldered, good at the use of the bow and arrows, with sinewy necks, and always holding their heads high in their pride. To sum up, these beings under the form of man hide the fierce nature of the beast.

That was a view very much coloured by race

prejudice and the superstitious fears of the time. It suggests that at a very early period of Balkan history the different races there had learned how to abuse one another. English readers might contrast it with Matthew Arnold's picture of a Tartar camp in *Sohrab and Rustum* :

    The sun by this had risen, and clear'd the fog
From the broad Oxus and the glittering sands.
And from their tents the Tartar horsemen filed
Into the open plain ; so Haman bade—
Haman, who next to Peran-Wisa ruled
The host, and still was in his lusty prime.
From their black tents, long files of horse, they stream'd ;
As when some grey November morn the files,
In marching order spread, of long-neck'd cranes
Stream over Casbin and the southern slopes
Of Elburz, from the Aralian estuaries,
Or some frore Caspian reed-bed, southward bound
For the warm Persian sea-board—so they stream'd.
The Tartars of the Oxus, the King's guard,
First, with black sheep-skin caps and with long spears ;
Large men, large steeds ; who from Bokhara come
And Khiva, and ferment the milk of mares.
Next, the more temperate Toorkmuns of the south,
The Tukas, and the lances of Salore,
And those from Attruck and the Caspian sands ;
Light men and on light steeds, who only drink
The acrid milk of camels, and their wells.
And then a swarm of wandering horse, who came
From far, and a more doubtful service own'd ;
The Tartars of Ferghana, from the banks
Of the Jaxartes, men with scanty beards

And close-set skull-caps; and those wilder hordes
Who roam o'er Kipchak and the northern waste,
Kalmucks and unkempt Kuzzaks, tribes who stray
Nearest the Pole, and wandering Kirghizzes,
Who come on shaggy ponies from Pamere;
These all filed out from camp into the plain.

Matthew Arnold gives to the Tartar camp tents of lattice-work, thick-piled carpets; to the Tartar leaders woollen coats, sandals, and the sheep-skin cap which is still the national headdress of the Bulgarians. More important, in proof of his idea of their civilisation, he credits them with a high sense of chivalry and a faithful regard for facts. *Sohrab and Rustum* is, of course, a flight of poetic fancy; but its "local colour" is founded on good evidence. Probably the Huns, despite the terrors of their name, the echoes of which still come down the corridors of time; despite the awful titles which their leaders won (such as Attila, "the Scourge of God"), were not on a very much lower plane of civilisation than the Goths with whom they fought, or with the other barbarians who tore at the prostrate body of the Roman Empire. One may see people of very much the same type to-day on the outer edges of Islam in some desert quarters; one may see and, if one has such taste for the wild

DEATH OF THE ROMAN EMPIRE 31

and the free in life as has Cunninghame Graham, one may admire:

There in the Sahara the wild old life, the life in which man and the animals seem to be nearer to each other than in the countries where we have changed beasts into meat-producing engines deprived of individuality, still takes its course, as it has done from immemorial time. Children respect their parents, wives look at their husbands almost as gods, and at the tent door elders administer what they imagine justice, stroking their long white beards, and as impressed with their judicial functions as if their dirty turbans or ropes of camels' hair bound round their heads, were horse-hair wigs, and the torn mat on which they sit a woolsack or a judge's bench, with a carved wooden canopy above it, decked with the royal arms.

Thus, when the blue baft-clad, thin, wiry desert-dweller on his lean horse or mangy camel comes into a town, the townsmen look on him as we should look on one of Cromwell's Ironsides, or on a Highlander, of those who marched to Derby and set King George's teeth, in pudding time, on edge.

The Huns' movement from the north-east was the first Asiatic invasion of Europe since the fall of the Persian Empire. Almost simultaneously with it the Saracen first entered from the south, as the ally of the Christian Emperor against the Goths; and another Gothic chronicler, Ammianus, tells how the Saracen warriors inspired also a lively horror in the Gothic mind. They came into battle almost naked, and having sprung upon a foe " with a hoarse and melancholy howl, sucked his life-blood from his throat." The Saracen of Ammianus was the forerunner of the Turk, the Hun of Jordanes, the forerunner of the Bulgarian. In neither case, of course, can the Gothic chronicler be accepted as an unprejudiced witness. But it is interesting to note how the first warriors from the Asiatic steppes impressed their contemporaries!

The first effect of the invasion of the country of the Goths by the Huns was to force the Goths to recross the Danube and trespass again on Roman territory. They sought leave from the Emperor Valens to do this. A contemporary historian records:

> The multitude of the Scythians escaping from the murderous savagery of the Huns, who spared not the life of woman or of child, amounted to not less than 200,000 men of fighting age [besides old men, women, and children]. These, standing upon the river-bank in a state of great excitement, stretched out their hands from afar with loud lamentations, and earnestly supplicated that they might be allowed to cross over the river, bewailing the calamity that had befallen them, and promising that they would faithfully adhere to the Imperial alliance if this boon were granted them.

A WOMAN OF THRACE, OF THE SHÔP TRIBE, AND OF MACEDONIA
The Shôps inhabit the Mountain District of Sofia

The Emperor Valens allowed the Gothic host to cross the Danube into Bulgaria and Thrace, and having given them shelter, starved them and treated them so harshly and cruelly that they were close to rebellion when another great Gothic host, under King Fritigern, crossed the Danube without leave and came down as far as Marcianople (now Schumla). Here he was entertained at a "friendly" banquet by the Roman general Lupicinus. But whilst the banquet was in progress disorder arose among the Goths and the Romans outside the hall. The Gothic historians tell :

News of this disturbance was brought to Lupicinus as he was sitting at his gorgeous banquet, watching the comic performers and heavy with wine and sleep. He at once ordered that all the Gothic soldiers, who, partly to do honour to their rank, and partly as a guard to their persons, had accompanied the generals into the palace, should be put to death. Thus, while Fritigern was at the banquet, he heard the cry of men in mortal agony, and soon ascertained that it proceeded from his own followers shut up in another part of the palace, whom the Roman soldiers at the command of their general were attempting to butcher. He drew his sword in the midst of the banqueters, exclaimed that he alone could pacify the tumult which had been raised among his followers, and rushed out of the dining-hall with his companions. They were received with shouts of joy by their countrymen outside; they mounted their horses and rode away, determined to revenge their slaughtered comrades.

Delighted to march once more under the generalship of one of the bravest of men, and to exchange the prospect of death by hunger for death on the battlefield, the Goths at once rose in arms. Lupicinus, with no proper preparation, joined battle with them at the ninth milestone from Marcianople, was defeated, and only saved himself by a shameful flight. The barbarians equipped themselves with the arms of the slain legionaries, and in truth that day ended in one blow the hunger of the Goths and the security of the Romans; for the Goths began thenceforward to comport themselves no longer as strangers but as inhabitants, and as lords to lay their commands upon the tillers of the soil throughout all the Northern provinces.

That began a war which inflicted the third great blow on the Roman Empire—the defeat and death of the Emperor Valens before Adrianople. The Goths in this campaign seem to have brought in some of their old enemies, the Huns, as allies—pretty clear proof of the contention I have set up that the Huns were not such desperate savages; but these Asiatics made the war rather more brutal than was usual for those days, without a doubt. Theodosius, the younger (son of that brave general who had just won back Britain for the Roman Empire), restored somewhat the

Roman power in the provinces south of the Balkans for a time. But in the year 380 the Romans made peace again with the Goths, allowing them to settle in Bulgaria as well as north of the Danube as allies of the Roman Power.

In the latter part of the fourth century and the first half of the fifth century the Huns fill the pages of Bulgarian history. Then came the Slavs; and then, in the seventh century, the Bulgars, almost certainly a Hun tribe, but Huns modified by two centuries of time. But the death of Valens may be said to have ended the Roman Empire as a World Power. Let us retrace our steps a little and give the chief facts as to how a Bulgarian Empire for a time—a very short time—replaced the Roman Empire over a great area of the Balkan Peninsula.

CHAPTER III

THE SCRAP-HEAP OF RACES

THE historian, rightly, must always march under a banner inscribed " Why ? " The facts of history bring no real informing to the human mind unless they can be traced to their causes, and thus a chain of events followed link by link to see why some happening was so fruitful in results, and to search for the relation of apparently isolated and accidental incidents.

The Balkan Peninsula has to-day just emerged from a most bloody war. It prepares for another to break out as soon as the exhaustion of the moment has passed. Since ever the pages of history were inscribed it has been vexed by savage wars. Why ?

There is an explanation near at hand and clear. In the Balkans there is a geographical area, which could house one nation comfortably, and is occupied by the scraps of half a dozen nations.

(1) There are the remnants of the Turks who at one time threatened the conquest of all Europe. Back from the walls of Vienna they have been driven little by little until now they occupy the toe only of the Balkan Peninsula. But the days have not far departed when they held almost all the Peninsula, and the present smallness of their portion dates back only from 1913.

(2) There are the Greeks, heirs of the traditions of Philip and Alexander, and of the old Roman Empire. For centuries their national but not their racial existence was dormant under the heel of the Turk. Greek independence was restored recently, and since the war of 1912–1913 has established itself vigorously.

(3) There are the Roumanians, descendants of the old Roman colony of Trajan in Dacia.

(4) There are the Bulgars, originally a Tartar people coming from the banks of the Volga, who entered Bulgaria in the seventh century as the Normans entered England at a later date, and who mingled with a Slav race they found there—at first as conquerors, afterwards becoming the absorbed race.

(5) There are the Serbs, somewhat akin to the Bulgars, whose original home seems to have been that of the Don Cossacks, who also came into the Peninsula in the seventh century. They are of purer Slav blood than the Bulgars.

(6) There are the Montenegrins, an off-shoot of the Serbs, who in the fourteenth century, when the Servian Empire fell, took to the hills and maintained their independence.

Those are the six main racial elements. But there are other scraps of peoples—the Albanians, for example, and the Macedonians, and tribes of Moslem Bulgars, and some Asiatic elements brought in by the Turks.

So far, then, the answer to the question, "Why are the Balkans so often at war?" is easy of answer. Given the existence on one peninsula of six different races, four of which have past great traditions of Empire, and there is certain to be uneasy house-keeping. But the inquiry has to be pushed further. Why is it that this unhappy Peninsula should have been made thus a scrap-heap for bits of nations, a refuge for sore-headed remnants of Imperial peoples? The answer to that is chiefly geographical.

A study of the map will show that when there

was a great movement from the north of Europe to the south, its easiest line of march was down the valley of the Danube along the Balkan Peninsula. In prehistoric times the peoples around the European shores of the Mediterranean brought to accomplishment a very advanced type of civilisation. It owed its foundations to Egypt or to the Semitic peoples, such as the Phoenicians, the Tyrians, and the Carthaginians, whose race-home was Asia Minor. Whilst this Mediterranean civilisation was being shaped in the south—in the north, in the forests or plains along the shores of the Baltic and of the North Sea, the fecund Teutonic people were swelling to a mighty host and overflowing their boundaries. A flood of these people in time came surging south searching for new lands. The natural course of that flood was by the valley of the Danube to the Balkan Peninsula. Down that peninsula they cut their path—not without bloodshed one may guess—and founded the Grecian civilisation. Of this prehistoric movement there is no written evidence; but it is accepted by anthropologists as certain. Thus Sir Harry Johnston records, not as a surmise but as a fact :

The Nordic races, armed with iron or steel swords, spears and arrow-heads, descended on the Alpine, Iberian, Lydian, and Aegean peoples of Southern Europe with irresistible strength. It was iron against bronze, copper, and stone; and iron won the day.

Prehistoric invasions of the Balkan Peninsula brought in the fair-haired, blue-eyed Greeks, the semi-barbarian conquerors of the Mukenaian and Minôan kingdoms. Tribes nearly allied to the Ancient Greeks diverged from them in Illyria, invaded the Italian Peninsula, and became the ancestors of the Sabines, Oscans, Latins, etc.

The parent ancestral speech of the German tribes about four to five thousand years ago was probably closely approximated in syntax, and in the form and pronunciation of words, to the other progenitors of European Aryan languages, especially the Lithuanian, Slav, Greek, and Italic dialects. Keltic speech was perhaps a little more different owing to its absorption of non-Aryan elements; but if we can judge of prehistoric German from what its eastern sister, the Gothic language, was like as late as the fifth century B.C., we can, without too much straining of facts, say that the prehistoric Greeks, when they passed across Hungary into the mountainous regions of the Balkans, and equally the early Italic invaders of Italy, were simply another branch of the Teutonic peoples later in separation than the Kelts, with whom, however, both the Italic and the Hellenic tribes were much interwoven. . . . Very English or German in physiognomy were most of the notabilities in the palmy days of Greece, to judge by their portrait-busts and the types of male and female beauty most in favour—as far south as Cyprus—in the periods when Greek art had become realistic and was released from the influence of an Aegean standard of beauty.

SISTOV, ON THE DANUBE

THE SCRAP-HEAP OF RACES

The invasion from the North of people flowing south by way of the Balkan Peninsula began that unhappy area's record of race-struggles and constant warfare. The Greek civilisation had scarcely established itself before it was attacked by an Asiatic Power—Persia. Again the Balkan Peninsula was inevitably the scene of the conflict, and such battles as Thermopylae and Marathon made names to resound for ever in the mouths of men. The peril from Persia over, the Balkan Peninsula, after seeing the struggles between the different Greek states for supremacy, was given another great ordeal of blood by Philip of Macedonia and Alexander the Great. Alexander carried a great invasion from Greece into the very heart of Asia, but founded no permanent empire.

The next phase of Balkan history was under the Roman Power. When the Roman strength had reached its zenith and entered upon the curve of decay, it was on the Balkan boundaries of the Empire that the main attack came. Finally, the rulers of the Roman Empire found it necessary to concentrate their strength close to the point of attack, and the capital was moved from Rome to Constantinople: the Roman

Empire became the Greek Empire. Thus, as we have seen in the previous chapter, the Balkan Peninsula was chosen as the arena in which an Empire founded in the Italian Peninsula was to die its long, uneasy death. The fate of this Greek Empire had been hardly decided when a new racial element came on the scene, and over the tottering Empire, already fighting fiercely with Bulgar and Serb for its small surviving patch of territory, strode the Turk in the full flush of his youthful strength, giving the last blow to the rule of the Caesars, and threatening all Christian Europe with conquest.

Made thus by the Fates the cockpit of the great struggles for World-Empire, the Balkan Peninsula was doomed to a bloody history: and the doom has not yet passed away. Perhaps it is some unconscious effect on the mind of the pity of this that makes the traveller to the Balkans feel so often a sympathy, almost unreasonable in intensity, for the Balkan peoples. The Balkan acres which they till are home to them. To civilisation those acres are the tournament field for the battles of races and nations.

What is now Bulgaria was in the days of Herodotus inhabited by Thracian and Illyrian tribes. They were united under the strong hand of Philip of Macedonia, and Bulgaria counts him the first great figure in her confused national history, and makes a claim to be the heir of his Macedonian Empire. The Romans appeared in Bulgaria during the period of the second war against Carthage. The Roman conquest of the Balkan country was slow, but shortly before the Christian era the Roman provinces of Moesia and Thracia comprised most of what is now Bulgaria.

In the days of Constantine, who removed the capital of his Empire to the Balkan Peninsula, Roman civilisation in what is now Bulgaria was already being swamped by barbarian invasions. The Goths and the Huns ravaged the land fiercely without attempting to colonise it. The Slavs were invaders of another type. They came to stay. It was at the beginning of the third century that the Slavs made their first appearance, and, crossing the Danube, began to settle in the great plains between the river and the Balkan Mountains. Later, they went southwards and formed colonies among the Thraco-Illyrians, the Roumanians, and the Greeks. This Slav occupation went on for several centuries.

In the seventh century of the Christian era a Hunnish tribe reached the banks of the Danube. It is known that this tribe came from the Volga and, crossing Russia, proceeded towards ancient Moesia, where it took possession of the whole north-east territory of the Balkans between the Danube and the Black Sea. These were the Bulgars, or Bolgars. The Slavs had already imposed on the races they had found in the Peninsula their language and customs. The Bulgars, too, assumed the language of the Slavs, and some of their customs. The Bulgars, however, gave their name to the mixed race, and assumed the political supremacy.

The analogy I have before suggested of the Norman invasion of England and the Bulgar invasion of Bulgaria generally holds good. The Slavs were a people who tilled the soil, cherished free institutions, fought on foot, were gentle in character. The Bulgars were nomads and pastoralists, obeying despotic chiefs, fighting as cavalry. They came as conquerors, but in time were absorbed in the more stable Slavonic type.

Without a doubt the Bulgars were racially nearly akin to the Turks—first cousins at least. Mingling with the Slavs they adopted their language and many of their customs. But something of the Turk survives to this day in the character of the Bulgarian people. It shows particularly in their treatment of their women. Though the Bulgarian is monogamic he submits his wife to an almost *harem* discipline. Once married she lives for the family alone. Though she does not wear a veil in the streets it is not customary for her to go out from her home except with her husband, nor to receive company except in his presence, nor to frequent theatres, restaurants, or other places of public amusement. There is thus no social life in Bulgaria in the European sense of the term, and there is great scope there for a campaign for " women's rights."

The Bulgars taking command over the Slav population in Bulgaria began a warfare against the enfeebled Greek Empire. That Empire gave up Moesia to the Bulgarian King, Isperich, and agreed to pay him a tribute, it being the custom of the degenerate descendants of the Roman Empire of the period thus to attempt to buy safety with bribes. The Emperor Justinian II. stopped this tribute, and a war followed, in which the Bulgarians were successful, and Justinian lost his throne and was driven to exile. Later,

Justinian made another treaty with the Bulgarians and offered his daughter in marriage to the new Bulgarian King, Tervel, and with Bulgarian help he was restored to his throne. But war between the Bulgars and the Empire was chronic. To quote a Bulgarian chronicler:

> The chief characteristics of the Bulgars were warlike virtues, discipline, patriotism, and enthusiasm. The Bulgarian kings brought their victorious armies to the gates of Constantinople, whose very existence they threatened. The Greek Emperor sought their friendship, and even consented to pay them tribute.

Bulgaria attained her greatest empire in the reign of King Kroum. Between King Isperich and King Kroum, however, Bulgaria had many ups and downs. The Bulgarian King, Kormisos, once almost reached the walls of Constantinople. But trouble among his own people prevented his victories being pushed home. Then a series of civil wars in Bulgaria weakened the nation, and a great section of it migrated to Asia Minor. The Roman Emperor, Constantine V., took this occasion to exact a full revenge for previous Bulgar attacks on Constantinople. The Bulgar army was routed, and an invading force carried the torch into every Bulgarian town. A new

THE SCRAP-HEAP OF RACES 47

Bulgar King, Cerig, restored his country's position somewhat by a secretly plotted massacre of all its enemies within its boundaries. The Empress Irene then ascended the Imperial throne at Constantinople and found herself unable to withstand the Bulgar power, and went back to the system of paying tribute to the Bulgarians as the price of safety.

King Kroum next ascended the throne of Bulgaria and, capable and savage warrior as he was, raised its power vastly. He defeated and slew the Greek Emperor, Nicephorus, in battle, and captured Sofia (809), the present capital of Bulgaria. Warfare was savage in those days, and between the Bulgars and the Greek emperors particularly savage. The defeated Imperial army was massacred to a man, from the Emperor down to the foot-soldier. King Kroum afterwards used the skull of the descendant of the Caesars as a drinking-cup.

A siege of Constantinople followed the defeat and death of the Emperor Nicephorus. The Bulgars affrighted the defenders of the city by their fierce orgies before the walls, by the human sacrifices they offered up in their sight, and by the resolute refusal of all quarter in the field.

The Empire tried to buy off the Bulgars with the promise of an annual tribute of gold, of cloth, and of young girls. The invaders finally retired with a great booty, and the death of King Kroum soon after relieved the anxiety of Constantinople.

Bulgaria seems now (the ninth century) to have suffered again from internal dissensions. These arose mostly out of religious issues. Many of the Slavs had become Christians, and some of the Bulgars also adopted the new faith. For a time the kings tried to crush out Christianity by persecutions, but in 864 the Bulgarian King, Boris, adopted Christianity—some say converted by his sister, who had been a prisoner of the Greeks and was baptized by them. His adherence to Christianity was announced in a treaty with the Greek Emperor, Michael III. Some of King Boris's subjects kept their affection for paganism and objected to the conversion of their king. Following the customs of the time they were all massacred, and Bulgaria became thus a wholly Christian kingdom.

King Boris, whom the Bulgarians look up to as the actual founder of the Bulgarian nation of to-day, hesitated long as to whether he should

ANCIENT COSTUME OF BALKAN PEASANT WOMEN
NEAR GABROVO

attach himself and his nation to the Roman or to the Greek branch of the Christian Church. He made the issue a matter of close bargaining. The Church was sought which was willing to allow to Bulgaria the highest degree of ecclesiastical independence, and which seemed to offer as the price of adhesion the greatest degree of political advantage.

At first the Greek Church would not allow Bulgaria to have a Patriarch of her own. King Boris sent, then, a deputation to Pope Nicholas at Rome, seeking if a better national bargain could be made there. Two bishops came over from Rome to negotiate. But in time King Boris veered back to a policy of attaching himself to the Greek Church, which now offered Bulgaria an Archbishop with a rank in the Church second only to that of the Greek Patriarch. In 869 Bulgaria definitely threw in her lot with the Greek Church.

Curiously those old religious controversies of the ninth century were revived in the nineteenth. Bulgaria has a persistent sense of nationalism, and looks upon religion largely in a national sense. In the ninth century her first care in changing her religion was to safeguard national interests. In the nineteenth century the first great concession she wrung from her Turkish masters was the setting up (1870) of a Bulgarian Exarch to be the official head of the Bulgarian Orthodox Church independent of the Greek Patriarch. A little later in the days of her freedom, when to her Roman Catholic ruler, King Ferdinand, was born a son (named Boris after the first Christian king of Bulgaria), the Bulgarians had him transferred in 1896 from the Roman to the Greek Church as a matter of national policy.

The controversy to-day between "Patriarchate" adherents of the Orthodox Church— *i.e.* Greeks, and the Exarchate adherents—*i.e.* Bulgarians, is perhaps the most bitter of all Balkan controversies. I have found it in places transcending far the religious gap between Turk and Christian, and in that particularly stormy North Macedonian corner of the Balkans a Patriarchate man gives first place in his hatred to an Exarchate man and second place to a Turk; and the Exarchate man reciprocates in like manner. Yet, as the Bulgarians insist, " the autonomous orthodox Bulgarian Church forms an inseparable part of the Holy Orthodox Church."

The Bulgarian Exarchate used to comprise all the Bulgarian dioceses in the provinces of the Turkish Empire, as they were enumerated explicitly or in general terms by the Firman of 1870 as well as the dioceses of the Bulgarian Principality. Most of the orthodox Bulgarian population in Turkey recognise the authority of the Exarchate, but some still owe allegiance to the Greek Patriarchate. What the religious position will be now that the wars of 1912–13 have changed boundaries so considerably it is hard to say. The Exarchate dioceses which used to be in Turkish territory but are now in Bulgarian territory, will, of course, pass into the main current of Bulgarian church life. But those Exarchate dioceses which have passed to Servia and to Greece will probably not find toleration.

King Boris of Bulgaria having raised his country to a great fame, and having endowed it with a rational church, retired to a monastery in 888 to make his peace with the next world. His son Vladimir succeeded to the throne, but ruled so unwisely that King Boris came back from the cloister to depose Vladimir and to set in his stead upon the throne Simeon, who created the first Bulgarian Empire.

CHAPTER IV

BULGARIA—A POWER AND A TURKISH PROVINCE

KING SIMEON reigned in Bulgaria thirty-four years, and raised his country during that time to the highest point of power it ever reached. Simeon had been educated at Constantinople and had learned all that the civilisation of the Grecian Empire could teach except a love and respect for the Grecian rule. He designed the overthrow of the tottering Grecian Empire, and dreamed of Bulgaria as the heir to the power of the Caesars.

When Simeon came to the throne, for many years the Grecian Empire and Bulgaria had been at peace. But a trade grievance soon enabled Simeon to enter upon a war against the feeble Greek Emperor then on the throne in Constantinople—Leo, known as the Philosopher. The Grecian forces were defeated and, following the ferocious Balkan custom of the times, the Grecian prisoners were all mutilated by having their noses cut off, and thus returned to their city. Constantinople in desperation appealed for help to the Magyars, who had recently burst into Europe from the steppes of Russia and occupied the land north of the Danube. The Magyars responded to the appeal, and at first were successful against the Bulgars, but King Simeon's strategy overcame them in the final stages of the campaign. He took advantage then of the temporary absence of their army in the west, and descended upon their homes in the region now known as Bessarabia and massacred all their wives and children. This act of savage cruelty drove the Magyars away finally from the Danube, and they migrated north and west to found the present kingdom of Hungary.

Relieved of the fear of the Magyars, King Simeon now attacked the Grecian Empire again, captured Adrianople, and laid siege to Constantinople. There were two emperors in the city then, in succession to Leo the Philosopher —Romanus Lecapenus and Constantine Porphyrogenitus. For all the grandeur of their names they rivalled one another in incompetency and timidity. Simeon was able to force upon the Grecian Empire a humiliating peace, which made Bulgaria now the paramount Power in the Balkans, since Servia had been already subdued by her arms. From the Roman Pope, Simeon received authority to be called "Czar of the Bulgarians and Autocrat of the Greeks." His capital at Preslav — now in ruins — was in his time one of the great cities of Europe, and a contemporary description of his palace says :

If a stranger coming from afar enters the outer court of the princely dwelling, he will be amazed, and ask many a question as he walks up to the gates. And if he goes within, he will see on either side buildings decorated with stone and wainscoted with wood of various colours. And if he goes yet farther into the courtyard he will behold lofty palaces and churches, bedecked with countless stones and wood and frescoes without, and with marble and copper and silver and gold within. Such grandeur he has never seen before, for in his own land there are only miserable huts of straw. Beside himself with astonishment, he will scarce believe his eyes. But if he perchance espy the prince sitting in his robe covered with pearls, with a chain of coins round his neck and bracelets on his wrists, girt about with a purple girdle and a sword of gold at his side, while on either hand his nobles are seated with golden chains, girdles, and bracelets upon them ; then will he answer when one asks him on his return home what he has seen :

A POWER AND A TURKISH PROVINCE 55

" I know not how to describe it; only thine own eyes could comprehend such splendour."

Under Simeon, art and literature flourished (in a Middle Ages sense) in Bulgaria; the Cyrillic alphabet—still used in Russia, Bulgaria, and Servia—had supplanted the Greek alphabet and had added to the growing sense of national consciousness. Simeon encouraged the production of books, and tradition credits him with having himself translated into the Slav language some of the writings of St. Chrysostom.

But all this Bulgarian prosperity had a serious check when Simeon died in 927 and the Czar Peter ascended the throne. Scarcely was Simeon cold in his grave before internal struggles had begun, owing to the jealousies of some of the nobles and their spirit of adventure. The boyars (knights) of Bulgaria had always had great authority. Now they took advantage of a monarch who was more suited for the cloister than the Court to revive old pretensions to independent power. Czar Peter turned to the Greek Empire for help, and sought to strengthen his position at home by a marriage with the grand-daughter of the Emperor Romanus Lecapenus. That policy served until a vigorous Greek Emperor came to the throne at Constantinople and set himself to avenge the victories of Simeon. The Greek Emperor called in the aid of the northern Russians against their kinsfolk the Bulgarian Slavs. There followed a typical Balkan year of war. The Russians succeeded only too well against the Bulgarians, and then the Greeks, in fear, joined with the Bulgarians to resist their further progress. Then the Servians took advantage of the war to shake off the Bulgarian suzerainty and regain their independence. An opposition party in Bulgaria, disgusted with the misfortunes which had befallen their country under Peter, added to these misfortunes by a revolt, and seceded to found the kingdom of Western Bulgaria under the boyar Shishman Mokar (963). To add to the troubles of the Balkans, the Bogomil heresy appeared, dividing further the strength of the Bulgarian nation. The Bogomils were the first of a long series of Slavonic fanatics, ancestors in spirit of the Doukhobors, the Stundists, and the Tolstoyans of our days, preaching the hermit life as the only truly holy one, forbidding marriage as well as war and the eating of meat. It was with such dissensions among the Christian states of the Balkans that

A WEDDING IN THE RHODOPES

A POWER AND A TURKISH PROVINCE 57

the way was prepared for the coming of the Turk to the Peninsula.

In 969 Boris II. followed Peter on the Bulgarian throne. He was faced by a new Russian invasion and by an attack from Czar David of Western Bulgaria. This latter attack he beat off, but was overwhelmed before the tide of Russian invasion and himself captured in battle. The Russians passed over Bulgaria to attack Constantinople, and that brought the Greeks into line with the Bulgarians to resist the invader. The Emperor John Zemissius made bold war upon the Russians, and captured from them their Bulgarian prisoner, the Czar Boris II. The Greek Emperor made no magnanimous use of his victory. He deposed the Bulgarian Czar and the Bulgarian Patriarch, emasculated the Czar's brother, and turned Bulgaria into a Greek province. Only in the rebel province of West Bulgaria did Bulgarian independence at this time survive, and from that province there arose in time a deliverer, the Czar Samuel, who was the fourth son of that boyar Shishman who founded the Western Bulgarian kingdom. At the beginning of his reign, in 976, Samuel had control only over the territory which is now known as

Macedonia, but soon he united to it all the old Empire of Bulgaria, and stretched the sway of his race over much of the land which is now comprised in Albania, Greece, and Servia. He began, then, a stern war with the Greek Emperor, Basil II., known to history as "the Bulgar-slayer," against whom is alleged a cruelty horrible even for the Balkans.

Capturing a Bulgarian army of over 10,000 men, Basil II. had all the soldiers blinded, leaving to each of their centurions, however, one eye, so that the mutilated men might be led back to their own country. A realistically horrible picture in the Sofia National Gallery commemorates this classic horror.

The war between the Czar Samuel and the Emperor Basil II. was marked by fluctuating fortunes. At first the Bulgarians were altogether successful, and in 981 Basil was so completely defeated that for fifteen years he was obliged to leave Samuel as the real master of the Balkan Peninsula. Then the tide turned. Near Thermopylae, Samuel was decisively defeated by the Greeks, and soon after found his Empire reduced to the dimensions of Albania and West Macedonia. War troubles that the Greeks had with

Asia brought to the Czar Samuel a brief respite, but a campaign in 1014—this was the one marked by the blinding of the captive Bulgarian army—shattered finally his power. He died that year heart-broken, it is said, at the sight of the return of his blinded army.

Thus, to quote a Bulgarian chronicle:

> In 1015 Bulgaria was brought to subjection. A new state of things began for the Bulgarians, who till then had never felt the control of an enemy. The people longed for liberty, and there were many attempts at revolt. Towards 1186, two brothers, John and Peter Assen, raised a revolt and succeeded in re-establishing the ancient kingdom, choosing as capital Tirnova, their native town. It was then that Tirnova became what it still remains, the historic town of Bulgaria. The reign of John and Peter Assen was a brilliant time for Bulgaria. Art and literature flourished as never before, and commerce developed to a considerable extent. Once more the Bulgarian Empire was respected and feared abroad.

But this Bulgarian Empire was doomed to as short a life as its predecessor, though for a brief while it held out the illusionary hope of permanency. Bulgaria, from the Danube to the Rhodope Mountains, was won from the Greeks, and John Assen was powerful enough to dream of entering into alliance with the Emperor

Frederick Barbarossa. An assassin's sword, however, ended John Assen's life prematurely. He was followed on the throne by his brother Peter. He, too, was assassinated, and was succeeded by his brother Kalojan, who had all the warlike virtues of John Assen, and re-established the Bulgarian Empire with territories which embraced more than half the whole Balkan Peninsula. Seeking to add to the reality of power some validity of title, Kalojan entered into negotiations with the Pope of Rome, made his submission to the Roman Church, and was crowned by a Papal nuncio as king.

It was about this time that Constantinople was captured by the Crusaders, and Count Baldwin of Flanders ascended the throne of the Caesars. The Greeks, driven from their capital but still holding some territory, made an alliance with Kalojan, and once again Greek and Bulgar fought side by side, defeating the Franks and taking the Emperor Baldwin prisoner. Then the alliance ended — never, it seems, can Bulgar and Greek be long at peace — and a war raged between the Greek Empire and Bulgaria, until in 1207 Kalojan was assassinated.

A brief period of prosperity continued for

Bulgaria while John Assen II. was on the throne. He was the most civilised and humane of all the rulers of ancient Bulgaria, and there is no stain of a massacre or a murder remembered against his name. He made wars reluctantly, but always successfully. An inscription in a church at Tirnova records his prowess :

In the year 1230, I, John Assen, Czar and Autocrat of the Bulgarians, obedient to God in Christ, son of the old Assen, have built this most worthy church from its foundations, and completely decked it with paintings in honour of the Forty holy Martyrs, by whose help, in the 12th year of my reign, when the church had just been painted, I set out to Roumania to the war and smote the Greek army and took captive the Czar Theodore Komnenus with all his nobles. And all lands have I conquered from Adrianople to Durazzo, the Greek, the Albanian, and the Servian land. Only the towns round Constantinople and that city itself did the Franks hold ; but these too bowed themselves beneath the hand of my sovereignty, for they had no other Czar but me, and prolonged their days according to my will, as God had so ordained. For without Him no word or work is accomplished. To Him be honour for ever. Amen.

John Assen II. was a great administrator as well as a great soldier. Whilst he declared the Church of Bulgaria independent, repudiating alike the Churches of Rome and of Constantinople, he tolerated all religions and gave sound encouragement to education. With his death passed away the last of the glory of ancient Bulgaria. Her story now was to be of almost unrelieved misfortune until the culminating misery of the Turkish conquest.

Internal dissensions, wars with the Venetians, the Hungarians, the Serbs, the Greeks, the Tartars,—all these vexed Bulgaria. The country became subject for a time to the Tartars, then recovered its independence, then came under the dominion of Servia after the battle of Kostendil (1330). The Servians, closely akin by blood, proved kind conquerors, and for some years the two Slav peoples of the Balkans kept peace by a common policy in which Bulgaria, if dependent, was not enslaved. But the Turk was rapidly pouring into Europe. In 1366 the Bulgarian Czar, Sisman III., agreed to become the vassal of the Turkish Sultan Murad, and the centuries of subjection to the Turk began. After the battle of Kossovo the grip of the Turk on Bulgaria was tightened. Tirnova was captured, the nobles of the nation massacred, the national freedom obliterated. The desire for independence barely survived. But there was one happy circumstance:

"It is a noteworthy fact," writes a Bulgarian authority, "that the Osmanlis, being themselves but little civilised, did not attempt to assimilate the Bulgarians in the sense in which civilised nations try to effect the intellectual and ethnic assimilation of a subject race. Except in isolated cases, where Bulgarian girls or young men were carried off and forced to adopt Mohammedanism, the Government never took any general measures to impose Mohammedanism or assimilate the Bulgarians to the Moslems. The Turks prided themselves on keeping apart from the Bulgarians, and this was fortunate for our nationality. Contented with their political supremacy and pleased to feel themselves masters, the Turks did not trouble about the spiritual life of the *rayas*, except to try to trample out all desires for independence. All these circumstances contributed to allow the Bulgarian people, crushed and ground down by the Turkish yoke, to concentrate and preserve their own inner spiritual life. They formed religious communities attached to the churches. These had a certain amount of autonomy, and, beside seeing after the churches, could keep schools. The national literature, full of the most poetic melancholy, handed down from generation to generation and developed by tradition, still tells us of the life of the Bulgarians under the Ottoman yoke. In these popular songs, the memory of the ancient Bulgarian kingdom is mingled with the sufferings of the present hour. The songs of this period are remarkable for the Oriental character of their tunes, and this is almost the sole trace of Moslem influence.

" In spite of the vigilance of the Turks, the religious associations served as centres to keep alive the national feeling. At the beginning of the nineteenth century, when Russia declared war against Turkey (1827), Bulgaria awoke."

From 1366 to 1827 Bulgaria had been enslaved by the Turk. Now within the space of a few days and with hardly an effort on her own behalf, she was suddenly to be restored to independence.

ROUSTCHOUK ON THE DANUBE

CHAPTER V

THE LIBERATION OF BULGARIA

SIGNIFICANTLY enough, the first sign of a renaissance of Bulgarian national feeling was an agitation not against the Turks but the Greeks. Patriotic Bulgarians, under the Sublime Porte, sought to re-establish their old National Church and shake it free from its subjection to the Greek Patriarch at Constantinople. The Sublime Porte was induced to look upon this demand with favour. A step which promised to emphasise the divisions between the Christians evidently should be of advantage to the Turks. The Greek Patriarch was urged to consent to the appointment of a Bulgarian bishop. He refused. In the face of that refusal Turkey acted as the creator of a new Christian Church, and in 1870 a firman of the Sultan created the Bulgarian Exarchate, and Bulgaria had again a national ecclesiastical organisation. Two years later the first Exarch was elected by the Bulgarian clergy. But gratitude for this religious concession did not extinguish the longings for political independence of the Bulgarian people. When a Christian insurrection broke out in Herzegovina against Turkey in 1875, the Bulgarian patriots rose in arms in different parts of their country. The massacres of Batak were the Turkish response, those "Bulgarian atrocities" which sent a shudder through all Europe and set a term to Turkish rule over the Christian populations in her European provinces.

I have been recently in the Balkans with the veteran war artist, Mr. Frederick Villiers, who has personal recollections of those times of massacre and atrocity. Speaking with him, an eye-witness of the devastation then wrought, it was possible to understand the fierce indignation with which the English-speaking world was stirred as the details of the horrors in the Balkans were unveiled. In all about 12,000 Bulgarian people perished, mostly butchered in cold blood. Turkish anger, it seems, was inflamed against the Bulgarians, because, in spite of the recent church concession, some of them had dared

"MYSTERY": A STUDY IN THE ROUSTCHOUK DISTRICT

THE LIBERATION OF BULGARIA 67

to strike for freedom; and this display of Turkish anger made the full freedom of Bulgaria certain.

At first an attempt had been made by the Powers to exert peaceful pressure upon Turkey, so that her Christian provinces should be granted local autonomy. The project of the Powers for Bulgaria proposed that the districts inhabited by Bulgarians should be divided into two provinces; the Eastern Province, with Tirnovo as capital, was to include the Sandjaks of Roustchouk, Tirnovo, Toultcha, Varna, Sliven, Philippopolis (not including Sultan-Eri and Ahi-Tchélebi), the kazas of Kirk Kilisse, Mustapha Pasha and Kasilagatch; and the Western Province, with Sofia as capital, the Sandjaks of Sofia, Vidin, Nisch, Uskub, Monastir, the three kazas of the north of Sérès, and the kazas of Stroumitza, Tikvesch, Velès, and Kastoria. Districts of from five to ten thousand inhabitants were to stand as the administrative unit. Christian and Mohammedans were to be settled homogeneously in these districts. Each district was to have at its head a mayor and a district council, elected by universal suffrage, and was to enjoy entire autonomy as regards local affairs. Several districts would form a Sandjak with a prefect at its head who was to be Christian or Mohammedan, according to the majority of the population of the Sandjak. He would be proposed by the Governor-General, and nominated by the Porte for four years.

Finally, every two Sandjaks were to be administered by a Christian Governor-General nominated by the Porte for five years, with consent of the Powers. He would govern the province with the help of a provincial assembly, composed of representatives chosen by the district councils for a term of four years, at the rate of one deputy to thirty or forty thousand inhabitants. This assembly would nominate an administrative council of ten members. The provincial assembly would be summoned every year to decide the budget and the taxes. The armed force was to be concentrated in the towns and there would be local militia beside. The language of the predominant nationality was to be employed, as well as Turkish. Finally, a Commission of International Control was to supervise the working of these proposals.

The Porte promised reforms on these lines, but did not go beyond promising. The task of

THE LIBERATION OF BULGARIA

forcing her to end a cruel tyranny was one for the battlefield.

The Russo-Turkish War broke out on April 12, 1877, and what Turkey had refused to yield of her own accord was wrested from her by force of arms, in the preliminary treaty of San Stefano. By this treaty, Bulgaria was made an autonomous principality subject to Turkey, with a Christian government and national militia. The Prince of Bulgaria was to be freely chosen by the Bulgarian people and accepted by the Sublime Porte, with the consent of the Powers. It was agreed that an assembly of notables, presided over by a Russian Commissioner and attended by a Turkish Commissioner, should meet at Philippopolis or Tirnovo before the election of the Prince to draw up a constitutional statute similar to those of the other Danubian principalities agreed to after the Treaty of Adrianople in 1830.

The Treaty of San Stefano brought into being on paper a Bulgaria greater in area than the Bulgaria of 1912, and greater even than the Bulgaria of 1914. But the Treaty was not ratified. Other European Powers, alarmed at the prospect of Russia becoming supreme in the

Balkans through the aid of a Bulgarian vassal state, interfered, and the Congress of Berlin substituted for the Treaty of San Stefano the Treaty of Berlin.

The Treaty of Berlin provided :

> Bulgaria is to be an independent Principality, subject to the Sultan, with a Christian government and a national militia ; the Prince of Bulgaria will be freely chosen by the Bulgarian nation and accepted by the Sublime Porte, with the approval of the Great Powers ; no member of a reigning European family can be elected Prince of Bulgaria ; in case of a vacancy of the throne the election will be repeated under the same conditions and with the same forms ; before the election of the Prince, an assembly of notables will decide on the constitutional statute of the Principality at Tirnovo. The laws will be based on principles of civil and religious liberty.

By the Treaty of Berlin the boundaries of Bulgaria were very greatly curtailed as compared with those of the Treaty of San Stefano, shrinking from an area as great almost as the Bulgarian Empire of Simeon down to a broad band of territory running between Eastern Roumelia and Roumania.

But the Bulgars kept the Treaty of San Stefano rather than the Treaty of Berlin before their eyes as their national charter. Almost from the first there were encroachments upon the pro-

A BLIND BEGGAR WOMAN

visions of the Treaty of Berlin. Its limitations of Bulgarian sovereignty were ignored little by little. Eastern Roumelia was united to Bulgaria proper by a bold and well-timed stroke. Another occasion was sought to get rid of the tribute to Turkey, and from a Prince, subject to a suzerain, the ruler of Bulgaria became a Czar, responsible to none but his subjects. Finally, when the war of 1912 against Turkey was entered upon to liberate further Christian provinces from the rule of the Turk, the Bulgarian people, if not the Bulgarian rulers, had clearly before their eyes the vision of the Bulgaria of the San Stefano Treaty. At one time it seemed as if that fond hope would be realised. But misfortunes and mistakes intervened, and as a final result of that and succeeding wars Bulgaria has been left with a comparatively small accession of territory, and is not much better off than she was in 1912.

It is not my purpose to attempt any detailed history of Bulgaria. I have designed, rather, an indication in broad outline of her national growth as a basis for, and an introduction to, an intimate picture of the country as it is to-day. All that is needed, then, to add to this chapter regarding the Liberation of Bulgaria, is that after the

Treaty of Berlin had been ratified, the first task that faced the principality of Bulgaria was to make it clear to Russia that, whilst she was grateful for the aid which had enabled her to become independent, she aspired to a real independence, and did not wish to exchange one master for another. The task was difficult, and caused some early trouble for the revived nation.

The first Prince chosen to be monarch of Bulgaria was Prince Alexander of Battenberg, a brave soldier but an indifferent statesman. He offended in turn both the Bulgarian patriots who wished him to lead their country to a complete freedom, and the Russians who would have her kept under a kind of tutelage to the " Little Father." Still Bulgaria, in his reign, made notable advances towards her national ideals. In 1885, obedient to the earnest wish of its inhabitants, Eastern Roumelia was incorporated with Bulgaria as a united principality, and that much of the Treaty of Berlin torn up. Turkey, whose rights were chiefly affected, decided not to make war upon this issue. The Great Powers, other than Russia, which had insisted, in the first instance, on the separation of Bulgaria into Bulgaria Proper and Eastern Roumelia because

A YOUNG MARRIED SHÔP WOMAN

THE LIBERATION OF BULGARIA 73

they feared that Bulgaria would be a mere appanage of Russia and would in actual effect bring the Russian frontier so much nearer to Constantinople, were now fairly reassured on that point. They not only made no protest, but they prevented Greece from doing so. There remained to be reckoned with only Russia and Servia. Russia showed her displeasure by recalling every Russian officer then serving with the Bulgarian army; but she did not make war. Servia, fearful that this Bulgarian aggrandisement jeopardised her own future in the Balkans, made war. Prince Alexander took the field with his troops—made up of Bulgarians, Macedonians, and Turks living in Bulgaria—and in the battle of Slivnitza Bulgaria won a decisive victory. She was not allowed to reap any direct fruits from it, as Austria interfered on behalf of Servia. The Treaty of Bucharest made peace without penalty to Servia, and Bulgaria was left with a greatly enhanced prestige as her sole reward.

It was a sad sequel to Prince Alexander's courage and address in this campaign that the next year he was deposed by a conspiracy in which the moving figures were the chiefs of the pro-Russian party in Bulgaria. The majority of the Bulgarians were not friendly to this revolution, and after the kidnapping of the Prince by the rebels a counter-revolution under Stambuloff would have restored him to the throne had it not been for the fact that he was irresolute in council though brave in the field. He could have won back his Crown, but chose rather to surrender it to Russia.

For some time after it was difficult to find a Prince for Bulgaria. The Crown was offered in turn to Prince Waldemar of Denmark and King Carol of Roumania. Finally, Prince Ferdinand of Saxe-Coburg-Gotha consented to embark on the great adventure of ruling Bulgaria. Wealthy, descended from the old French royal house on his mother's side, and connected with the Austrian and German royal houses on his father's, handsome and youthful, Prince Ferdinand had splendid qualifications for his new responsibility. He showed, too, from the outset, a fine diplomatic skill and successfully steered his country through the perilous days which followed his accession. Russia at first refused to sanction the choice of him as Prince, and that involved the other Powers in a policy of refusing him "recognition." He was thus, in a sense, a boycotted monarch.

A BULGARIAN MARKET TOWN

THE LIBERATION OF BULGARIA 75

With steady and patient skill Prince Ferdinand worked to overcome the obstacles which stood in the way of Bulgarian national aspirations, aided much by the masterful statesmanship of Stambuloff. A good understanding was come to with Turkey, still Bulgaria's suzerain power, and in 1890 Turkey made the important concession to Bulgaria of appointing Bulgarian bishops in Macedonia. In 1893 Prince Ferdinand married Princess Marie Louise of Parma, and the next year an heir was born to them, Prince Boris. A reconciliation with Russia followed.

Bulgaria now made steady and peaceful progress, the only cloud on her sky the sorrows of her co-religionists in Macedonia. In 1908 advantage was taken of the " Young Turk " revolution in Turkey for the Bulgarian Prince to denounce all allegiance to Turkey, and Bulgaria was declared fully independent and Ferdinand was crowned at Tirnovo as Czar of the Bulgarians. Turkey was not able to protest, and her confessed weakness nourished to powerful strength the general desire of the Christian peoples in the Balkans to free their co-religionists in Thrace and Macedonia from the rule of the Moslem. " The Balkan League " was formed, and Bulgaria,

Greece, Montenegro, and Servia prepared to force from Turkey by war what the Great Powers had so far failed to secure by diplomacy—the relief of Macedonia from oppression and misrule. It was during the war of 1912–13 that I had an opportunity of studying the Bulgarian people at close hand, as I accompanied the Bulgarian forces as war correspondent.

CHAPTER VI

THE WAR OF 1912-13

I CAN still recollect the glad surprise which a first sight of Sofia gave to me. With the then conventional view of the Balkan states, I had expected, on leaving Buda-Pesth, to cut away altogether from civilisation. Paved streets; solid and good, if not exactly handsome, buildings; first-class hotels and cafés; electric trams and comfortable, cheap cabs; luxurious public baths; well-stocked stores; a telephone system, water-supply, drainage — each one of these was a surprise. I had expected a semi-barbaric Eastern town. I found a modern capital, small but orderly, clean, and well managed.

That enthusiastic friend of the Balkan nationalities, Mr. Noel Buxton, M.P., writing of Sofia and other Balkan capitals, becomes quite lyrical in his praise:

"Their capitals," he writes, "have at all times an aspect of reality, industry, and simplicity. There is little needless wealth to show, and nothing which, in the West, would be called luxury. Every one is a worker, and every one a serious politician. There are no drones, and none who spend their lives in the pleasures, refinements, luxuries, vices, the idle amusements of the great cities of Europe. The buildings represent utility, means fairly adapted to ends, but with no cumbrous decoration or ponderous display. These capitals are bureaucratic settlements, devoted to the deliberate ends of national government with a minimum of waste, strictly appropriated to use alone, rendering their service to the nation as a counting-house renders its service to a great factory. Peasants walk their streets in brilliant village dresses. No one thinks a rational country costume inappropriate to the pavement of the capital. This is an index to the idea of purpose which pervades the town; there is none of the sense that a different costume is needed for urban life, an idea which arises from the association of towns with pleasure and display.

"Few sights can be more inspiring to the lover of liberty and national progress than a view of Sofia from the hill where the great seminary of the national church overlooks the plain. There at your feet is spread out the unpretentious seat of a government which stands for the advance of European order in lands long blighted with barbarism. Here resides, and is centred, the virile force of a people which has advanced the bounds of liberty. From here, symbolised by the rivers and roads running down on each side, has extended, and will further extend, the power of modern education, of unhampered ideas, of science and of humanity. From this magnificent view-point Sofia stretches along the low

BLESSING THE LAMB ON ST. GEORGE'S DAY

hill with the dark background of the Balkan beyond. Against that background now stands out the new embodiment of Bulgarian and Slavonic energy, genius, and freedom of mind, the great cathedral, with its vast golden domes brilliantly standing out from the shade behind them. In no other capital is a great church shown to such effect, viewed from one range of hills against the mountainous slopes of another. It is a building which, with its marvellous mural paintings, would in any capital form an object of world interest, but which, in the capital of a tiny peasant State, supremely embodies that breadth of mind which

> . . . rejects the lore
> Of nicely calculated less or more.

I confess humbly that I could not see all that in Sofia. But the city was a welcome surprise, recalling Turin in its situation beneath a great range of mountains, in its size and its general disposition. With closer acquaintance, which came to me during the armistice that followed the first phase of the war, Sofia showed as still clean, well managed, admirable, but, oh, so deadly dull. The system of partial seclusion of the womenfolk kills all social life, and the absence of a feminine element in the restaurants and other places of social resort deprives them of all convivial charm. One could eat, drink, work in Sofia, and that was all.

Coming first to Sofia just as war had been declared, I was struck by the evidence of the exceedingly careful preparation that the Bulgarians had made for the struggle. This was no unexpected or sudden war; they had known for some time that war was inevitable; for they had made up their minds for quite a considerable time that the wrongs of their fellow-nationals in Macedonia and Thrace would have to be righted by force of arms. Attempts on the part of the Powers to enforce reforms in the Christian provinces of Turkey had, in the opinion of the Bulgars, been absolute failures. In their opinion there was nothing to hope for except armed intervention on their part against Turkey. And, believing that, they had made most careful preparation, extending over several years, for this struggle.

That preparation was in every sense admirable. For instance, it had extended, I gathered from informants in Bulgaria, to this degree, that they formed military camps in winter for the training of their troops. Thus they did not train solely in the most favourable time of the year for manœuvres, but in the unfavourable weather too, in case that time should prove favourable for their war. I think the standard of their artillery

THE CATHEDRAL, SOFIA

arm, and the evidence of the scientific training of their officers, prove to what extent their training beforehand had gone. Most of the officers in high command I met at the front had been trained at the Military College at St. Petrograd, some of them at the Military College at Turin, and others again at a Military College which had been established at Sofia. Of this last-named the head was Colonel Jostoff, who was Chief-of-Staff to General Demetrieff (the great conquering general of this war), and a singularly able soldier. He was the chief Professor of the Military College at Sofia, and judging by the standard he set, the Military College must have reached a high degree of efficiency.

The Balkan League having been formed, and the time being ripe for the war, Bulgaria was quite determined that war should be. The Turks at that time were inclined to make reforms and concessions; they had an inclination to ease the pressure on their Christian subjects in the Christian provinces. Perhaps knowing—perhaps not knowing—that they were unready for war themselves, but feeling that the Balkan States were preparing for war, the Turks were undoubtedly willing to make great concessions. But whatever concessions the Turks might have offered, war would still have taken place.

I do not think one need offer any harsh criticism about a nation coming to such a decision as that. If you have made your preparation for war—perhaps a very expensive preparation, perhaps a preparation which has involved very great commitments apart from expense—it is not reasonable to suppose that at the last moment you will consent to stop that war.

I was much struck with the wonderful value to the Bulgarian generals of the fact that the whole Bulgarian nation was filled with the martial spirit —was, in a sense, wrapped up in the colours. Every male Bulgarian citizen was trained to the use of arms. Every Bulgarian citizen of fighting age was engaged either at the front or on the lines of communication. Before the war, every Bulgarian man, being a soldier, was under a soldier's honour; and the preliminaries of the war, the preparations for mobilisation in particular, were carried out with a degree of secrecy that, I think, astonished every Court and every Military Department in Europe. The secret was so well kept that one of the diplomatists in Roumania left for a holiday three days before the declaration

THE WAR OF 1912-13

of war, feeling certain that there was to be no war.

Bulgaria has a newspaper Press that, on ordinary matters, for delightful irresponsibility, might be matched in London. Yet not a single whisper of what the nation was designing and planning leaked abroad. Because the whole nation was a soldier, and the whole nation was under a soldier's honour, absolute secrecy could be kept. No one abroad knew anything, either from the babbling of " Pro-Turks," or from the newspapers, that this great campaign was being designed by Bulgaria.

The Secret Service of Bulgaria before the war had evidently been excellent. They seemed to know all that was necessary to know about the country in which they were going to fight; and I think this very complete knowledge of theirs was in part responsible for the arrangements which were made between the Balkan Allies for carrying on the war. The Bulgarian people had made up their minds to do the lion's share of the work and to have the lion's share of the spoils, for the Bulgarian people knew the state of corruption and rottenness to which the Turkish nation had come. When I reached Sofia, the Bulgarians told me they were going to be in Constantinople three weeks after the declaration of war. That was the view that they took of the possibilities of the campaign. And they kept their programme as far as Chatalja fairly closely.

Having declared war, the Bulgarians invaded Turkey along two main lines, by the railway which passed through Adrianople to Constantinople and by the wild mountain passes of the north between Yamboli and Kirk Kilisse. There was great enterprise shown in this second line of advance and it was responsible for all the great victories won. Taking Kirk Kilisse by surprise the Bulgarian forces kept the Turkish vanguard on the run until Lule Burgas, where the Turkish main army made a stand and the decisive battle of the campaign was fought. The Turks were utterly routed and fled in confusion towards Constantinople by Tchorlu. Had an enterprising pursuit on the part of the Bulgarians been possible, the Bulgarian army undoubtedly would have then entered Constantinople and the Christmas Mass would have been said at St. Sophia. But the strength of the Bulgarian attack was exhausted by the tremendous exertions of marching and fighting which they had already made and a long pause to recuperate was necessary. That pause enabled the Turks to re-marshal their forces and to make a stand at the fortified lines of Chatalja some twenty miles as the crow flies from Constantinople. Against those lines a Bulgarian attack was finally launched, but too late. The entrenched Turks were strong enough to withstand the attack of the Bulgarian forces. My diary of these three critical days of the campaign reads :

ERMENIKIOI
(Headquarters of the Third Bulgarian Army),
November 17 (*Sunday*).

The battle of Chatalja has been opened. To-day, General Demetrieff rode out with his staff to the battlefield whilst the bells of a Christian church in this little village rang. The day was spent in artillery reconnaissance, the Bulgarian guns searching the Turkish entrenchments to discover their real strength. Only once during the day was the infantry employed; and then it was rather to take the place of artillery than to complete the work begun by artillery. It seems to me that the Bulgarian forces have not enough big gun ammunition at the front. They are ten days from their base and shells must come up by ox-waggon the greater part of the way.

ERMENIKIOI, *November* 18.

This was a wild day on the Chatalja hills. Driving rain and mist swept over from the Black Sea, and at times obscured all the valley across which the battle raged. With but slight support from the artillery the

Bulgarian infantry was sent again and again up to the Turkish entrenchments. Once a fort was taken but had to be abandoned again. The result of the day's fighting is indecisive. The Bulgarian forces have driven in the Turkish right flank a little, but have effected nothing against the central positions which bar the road to Constantinople. It is clear that the artillery is not well enough supplied with ammunition. There is a sprinkle of shells when there should be a flood. Gallant as is the infantry it cannot win much ground faced by conditions such as the Light Brigade met at Balaclava.

ERMENIKIOI, *November* 19.

Operations have been suspended. Yesterday's cold and bitter weather has fanned to an epidemic the choleraic dysentery which had been creeping through the trenches. The casualties in the fighting had been heavy. " But for every wounded man who comes to the Hospitals," Colonel Jostoff, the chief of the staff, tells me, " there are ten who say ' I am ill.' " The Bulgarians recognise bitterly that in their otherwise fine organisation there has been one flaw, the medical service. Among this nation of peasant proprietors—sturdy, abstemious, moral, living in the main on wholemeal bread and water—illness was so rare that the medical service was but little regarded. Up to Chatalja confidence in the rude health of the peasants was justified. They passed through cold, hunger, fatigue and kept healthy. But ignorant of sanitary discipline, camped among the filthy Turkish villages, the choleraic dysentery passed from the Turkish trenches to theirs. There are 30,000 cases of illness and the healthy for the first time feel fear as they see the torments of the sick. The Bulgarians recognise that there must be a pause in the fighting whilst the hospital and sanitary service is reorganised.

There was this check, mainly because, in an otherwise perfect system of training, sanitation had been overlooked. From a military point of view, of course, it was almost impossible in any case that the Bulgarian army should have forced the Chatalja lines without a railway line to bring up ammunition from their base. It was, however, an army which had been accustomed to do the impossible. But for the cholera I believe it might have got through to the walls of Constantinople.

During the latter part of 1913 there was a chorus of unstinted praise in Europe of Bulgarian strategy. Candidly I cannot agree entirely with some of the views then expressed, which, to me, seem to have been inspired not so much by a study of the Bulgarian strategy, as by admiration of the wonderful heroism and courage of the soldiers. At the outset Bulgarian generalship was exceedingly good; the reconnaissance phase of the campaign was carried through perfectly. In that the soldier was assisted by the perfect discipline of the nation, which allowed a cheerful obedience to the most exacting demands and absolute secrecy. But it seemed to me that at the stage when the battle of Lule Burgas had been fought and won, there was a very serious mistake. (I am not writing now in the light of the ultimate result, for I expressed this view to Mr. Prior, of the London *Times*, in voyaging with him from Mustapha Pasha to Stara Zagora in November 1913.) There was a very serious mistake in the policy of " masking " Adrianople. I have reasons for thinking that that was not the original plan of the soldiers. Their strategy was, in the first instance, to deceive the Turks as to where the blow was to come from. And in that they succeeded admirably. No one knew where the main attack on the frontier would be made. It was made unexpectedly at Kirk Kilisse, when all expectation was that it would be made through Mustapha Pasha and towards Adrianople. But after that period of secrecy, when the main attack developed, and the Turks knew where the Bulgarian forces were, it seemed to me it was a great mistake for the Bulgarian army to push on as they did, leaving Adrianople in their rear.

It was not merely that Adrianople was a fortress, but it was a fortress which straddled their one line of communication. The railway from

AN ADRIANOPLE STREET
Over the roofs, the spiral minaret of Bourmali Jami,
white marble and red granite

Sofia to Constantinople passed through Adrianople. Except for that railway there was no other railroad, and there was no other carriage road, one might say, for the Turk did not build roads. Once you were across the Turkish frontier you met with tracks, not roads.

The effect of leaving Adrianople in the hands of the enemy was that supplies for the army in the field coming from Bulgaria could travel by one of two routes. They could come through Yamboli to Kirk Kilisse, or they could come through Novi Zagora to Mustapha Pasha by railway, and then to Kirk Kilisse around Adrianople. From Kirk Kilisse to the rail-head at Seleniki, close to Chatalja, they could come not by railway but by a tramway, a very limited railway. If Adrianople had fallen, the railway would have been open. The Bulgarian railway service had, I think, something over one hundred powerful locomotives at the outset of the war, and whilst it was a single line in places, it was an effective line right down to as near Constantinople as they could get. But, Adrianople being in the hands of the enemy, supplies coming from Yamboli had to travel to Kirk Kilisse by track, mostly by bullock wagon, and that journey took five, six, or seven days.

The British Army Medical Detachment travelling over that road took six days.

If one took the other road one got to Mustapha Pasha comfortably by railway. And then it was necessary to use bullock or horse transport from Mustapha Pasha to Kirk Kilisse. That journey I took twice; once with an ox-wagon, and afterwards with a set of fast horses, and the least period for the journey was five days. From Kirk Kilisse there was a line of light railway joining the main line. But on that line the Bulgarians had only six engines, and, I think, thirty-two carriages; so that, for practical purposes, the railway was of very little use indeed past Mustapha Pasha. Whilst Adrianople was in the hands of the enemy, the Bulgarians had practically no line of communication.

My reason for believing that it was not the original plan of the generals to leave Adrianople " masked " is, that in the first instance I have a fairly high opinion of the generals, and I do not think they could have designed that; but I think rather it was forced upon them by the politicians saying, " We must hurry through, we must attempt something, no matter how desperate it is, something decisive." But, apart from the high opinion I have of the Bulgarian generals, the fact remains that after Adrianople had been attacked in a very half-hearted way, and after the main Bulgarian army had pushed on to the lines of Chatalja, the Bulgarians called in the aid of a Servian division to help them against Adrianople. I am sure they would not have done that if it had not been their wish to subdue Adrianople.

The position of the Bulgarian army on the lines of Chatalja with Adrianople in the hands of the enemy was this, that it took practically their whole transport facilities to keep the army supplied with food, and there was no possibility of keeping the army properly supplied with ammunition. So if the Bulgarian generals had really designed to carry the lines of Chatalja without first attacking Adrianople, they miscalculated seriously. But I do not think they did. It was probably a plan forced upon them by political authority, feeling that the war must be pushed to a conclusion somehow. Why the Bulgarians did not take Adrianople quickly in the first place is, I think, to be explained simply by the fact that they could not. But if their train of sappers had been of the same kind of stuff as their field artillery, they could have taken Adrianople in the first week of the war.

The Bulgarians had no effective siege-train. A press photographer at Mustapha Pasha was very much annoyed because photographs he had taken of guns passing through the towns were not allowed to be sent through to his paper. He sent a humorous message to his editor, that he could not send photographs of guns, " it being a military secret that the Bulgarians had any guns." But the reason the Bulgarians did not want photographs taken was that these guns were practically useless for the purpose for which they were intended.

The main excellence of the Bulgarian army was its infantry, which was very steady under punishment, admirably disciplined, perfect in courage, and which had, I think, that supreme merit in infantry, that it always wanted to get to work with the bayonet. The Bulgarian soldiers had a joke among themselves. The order for " Bayonets forward ! " was, as near as I could get it, " *Nepret nanochi.*" Arguing by similarity of sound, the Bulgarian soldier affected to believe it meant " Spit five men on your bayonet." It was the common camp saying that it was the duty of the infantryman to impale five Turks on his bayonet, to show that he had conducted himself well. The Bulgarian infantrymen had devised a little " jim " in regard to bayonet work, which I had not heard of being used in war before. When they were in the trenches, and the order was expected to fix bayonets, they had a habit of fixing them, or rather pretending to, with a tremendous rattle, on which signal the Turks would often leave their trenches and run, expecting the bayonet charge; but the Bulgarians still stuck to their trenches, and got in another volley.

The artillery work of the Bulgarians was very good indeed; they had an excellent field-piece, practically the same field-piece as the French army. Their work was very fine with regard to aim and to the bursting of shrapnel, and their firing from concealed positions was also good. But I never saw enterprising work on their part; I never saw them go into the open, except during a brief time at Chatalja. They seemed to dig themselves in behind the crest of a hill, where they could fire, unobserved by the enemy.

Now, with regard to the conduct of the troops. Much has been said about outrages in this war.

I believe that in Macedonia, where irregular troops were at work, outrages were frequent on both sides; but in my observation of the main army there was a singular lack of any excess. The war, as I saw it, was carried out by the Bulgarians under the most humane possible conditions. At Chundra Bridge I was walking across country, and I had separated myself from my cart. I arrived at the bridge at eight o'clock at night, and found a vedette on guard. They took me for a Turk. I had on English civilian green puttees, and green was the colour of the Turks. It was a cold night, and I wished to take refuge at the camp fire, waiting for my cart to come. Though they thought I was a Turk, they allowed me to stay at their camp fire for two hours. Then an officer who could speak French appeared, and I was safe; the men attempted in no way to molest me during those two hours. They made signs as of cutting throats, and so on, but they were doing it humorously, and they showed no intention to cut mine. Yet I was there irregularly, and I could not explain to them how I came to be there.

The extraordinary simplicity of the commissariat helped the Bulgarian generals a great deal. The men had bread and cheese, sometimes even bread alone; and that was accounted a satisfactory ration. When meat and other things could be obtained, they were obtained; but there were long periods when the Bulgarian soldier had nothing but bread and water. (The water, unfortunately, he took wherever he could get it, by the side of his route at any stream he could find. There was no attempt to ensure a pure water supply for the army.) I do not think that without the simplicity of commissariat it would have been possible for the Bulgarian forces to have got as far as they did. There was an entire absence of tinned foods. If you travelled in the trail of the Bulgarian army, you found it impossible to imagine that an army had passed that way; because there was none of the litter which is usually left by an army. It was not that they cleared away their rubbish with them; it simply did not exist. Their bread and cheese seemed to be a good fighting diet.

The transport was, naturally, the great problem which faced the generals. I have already said something about the extreme difficulty of that transport. I have seen at Seleniki, which is the point at which the rail-head was, within thirty miles of Constantinople as the crow flies, ox-wagons, which had come from the Shipka Pass, in the north of Bulgaria. I asked one driver how long he had been on the road; he told me three weeks. He was carrying food down to the front.

The way the ox-wagons were used for transport was a marvel of organisation to me. The transport officer at Mustapha Pasha, with whom I became very friendly, was lyrical in his praise of the ox-wagon. It was, he said, the only thing that stuck to him during the war. The railway got choked, and even the horse failed, but the ox never failed. There were thousands of ox-wagons crawling across the country. These oxen do not walk, they crawl, like an insect, with an irresistible crawl. It reminded me of those armies of soldier ants which move across Africa, eating everything which they come across, and stopping at nothing. I had an ox-wagon coming from Mustapha Pasha to Kirk Kilisse, and we went over the hills and down through the valleys, and stopped for nothing—we never had to unload once.

And one can sleep in those ox-wagons. There is no jumping and pulling at the traces, such as you get with a harnessed horse. The ox-wagon moved slowly; but it always moved. If the ox-transport had not been so perfectly organised,

THE SHIPKA PASS

and if the oxen had not been so patiently enduring as they proved to be, the Bulgarian army must have perished by starvation.

And yet at Mustapha Pasha a Censor would not allow us to send anything about the ox-wagons. That officer thought the ox-cart was derogatory to the dignity of the army. If we had been able to say that they had such things as motor transport, or steam wagons, he would have cheerfully allowed us to send it.

After Lule Burgas the ox-transport had to do the impossible. It was impossible for it to maintain the food and the ammunition supply of the army at the front, which I suppose must have numbered 250,000 to 300,000 men. That army had got right away from its base, with the one line of railway straddled by the enemy, and with the ox as practically the only means of transport.

The position of the Bulgarian nation towards its Government on the outbreak of the war is, I think, extremely interesting as a lesson in patriotism. Every man fought who could fight. But further, every family put its surplus of goods into the war-chest. The men marched away to the front; and the women of the house loaded up the surplus goods which they had in the house, and brought them for the use of the military authorities on the ox-wagons, which also went to the military authorities to be used on requisition.

A Bulgarian law, not one which was passed on the outbreak of the war—they were far too clever for that—but an Act which was part of the organic law of the country, allowed the military authorities to requisition all surplus food and all surplus goods which could be of value to the army on the outbreak of hostilities. The whole machinery for that had been provided beforehand. But so great was the voluntary patriotism of the people that this machinery practically had not to be used in any compulsory form. Goods were brought in voluntarily, wagons, cart-horses, and oxen, and all the surplus flour and wheat, and—I have the official figures from the Bulgarian Treasurer—the goods which were obtained in this way totalled in value some six million pounds. The Bulgarian people represent half the population of London. The population is poor. Their national existence dates back only half a century. But they are very frugal and saving; that six millions which the Government signed for represented practically all the savings which the Bulgarian people had at the outbreak of the war.

CHAPTER VII

A WAR CORRESPONDENT'S TRIALS IN BULGARIA

A SENSE of grievance was the first fruits of my experience as a war correspondent in Bulgaria. It was the general policy of the Bulgarian army and the Bulgarian military authorities to prevent war correspondents seeing anything of their operations. They wished nothing to interfere with the secrecy of their plans. There were only three British journalists who succeeded, in the ultimate result, in getting to the front and seeing the final battle of the first phase of the war, at Chatalja. There were over a hundred correspondents who attempted to go. Perhaps as I was one of three who succeeded, I do not think I, personally, have any reason to complain. But I found a good deal of vexation in the Bulgarian policy, which was to prevent any knowledge of their plans, their dispositions, their strategy, and their tactics, from getting beyond the small circle of their own General Staff. Even some of their generals in the field were kept in partial ignorance. Officers of high standing, unless they were on the General Staff, knew little of the general plan; they were informed only about the particular operations in which they were engaged.

This policy of secrecy was, however, a good thing from the point of view of getting to know the Bulgarian people. If the military authorities had given me facilities to go with the army and see its operations I should have become familiar with the Headquarters Staff, perhaps with a few regimental officers, but not with the great mass of the army nor with the Bulgarian people generally. But the refusal of facilities to accompany the army cast upon me the responsibility of trying to get through somehow to the front, and in the process of getting through I won to knowledge of the peasant soldiers and their home life.

Ultimately the residuum of my grievance was not with the secretive methods of the Bulgarians —they were wise and necessary—but with the wild fictions which some correspondents thought to be the proper response to that policy of secretiveness.

Returned to Kirk Kilisse from the Bulgarian lines at Chatalja, I amused myself in an odd hour with burrowing among a great pile of newspapers in the Censor's office, and reading here and there the war news from English, French, and Belgian papers.

Dazed, amazed, I recognised that I had seemingly mistaken the duties of a war correspondent. For some six weeks I had been following an army in breathless, anxious chase of facts; wheedling Censors to get some few of those facts into a telegraph office; learning then, perhaps, that the custom at that particular telegraph office was to forward telegrams to Sofia, a ten days' journey, by bullock-wagon and railway, to give them time to mature. Now here, piping hot, were the stories of the war.

There was the vivid story of the battle of Chatalja. This story was started seven days too soon; had the positions and the armies all wrong; the result all wrong; and the picturesque details were in harmony. But for the purposes of the public it was a very good story of a battle. Those men who, after great hardships, were enabled to see the actual battle found that the poor messages which the Censor permitted them to send took ten days or more in transmission to London. Why have taken all the trouble and expense of going to the front? Buda-Pesth, on the way there, is a lovely city; Bucharest also; and charming Vienna was not at all too far away if you had a good staff-map and a lively military imagination.

In yet another paper there was a vivid picture —scenery, date, Greenwich time, and all to give an air of artistic verisimilitude—of the signing of the Peace armistice. The armistice had not been signed at the time, was not signed for some days after. But it would have been absurd to have waited, since " our special correspondent " had seen it all in advance, right down to the embrace of the Turkish delegate and the Bulgarian delegate, and knew that some of the conditions were that the Turkish commissariat was to feed the Bulgarian troops at Chatalja and the Bulgarian commissariat the Turkish troops in Adrianople. If his paper had waited for the truth that most charming story would never have seen the light.

So, in a little book I shall one day bring out

in the " Attractive Occupations " series on " How to be a War Correspondent," I shall give this general advice :

1. Before operations begin, visit the army to which you are accredited, and take notes of the general appearance of officers and men. Also learn a few military phrases of their language. Ascertain all possible particulars of a personal character concerning the generals and chief officers.

2. Return then to a base outside the country. It must have good telegraph communication with your newspaper. For the rest you may decide its locality by the quality of the wine, or the beer, or the cooking.

3. Secure a set of good maps of the scene of operations. It will be handy also to have any books which have been published describing campaigns over the same *terrain.*

4. Keep in touch with the official bulletins issued by the military authorities from the scene of operations. But be on guard not to become enslaved by them. If, for instance, you wait for official notices of battles, you will be much hampered in your picturesque work. Fight battles when they ought to be fought and

how they ought to be fought. The story's the thing.

5. A little sprinkling of personal experience is wise ; for example, a bivouac on the battlefield, toasting your bacon at a fire made of a broken-down gun-carriage with a bayonet taken from a dead soldier. Mention the nationality of the bacon. You cannot be too precise in details.

Ko-Ko's account of the execution of Nankipoo is, in short, the model for the future war correspondent. The other sort of war correspondent, who patiently studied and recorded operations, seems to be doomed. In the nature of things it must be so. The more competent and the more accurate he is, the greater the danger he is to the army which he accompanies. His despatches, published in his newspaper and telegraphed promptly to the other side, give to them at a cheap cost that information of what is going on *behind* their enemy's screen of scouts which is so vital to tactical, and sometimes to strategical, dispositions. To try to obtain that information an army pours out much blood and treasure ; to guard that information an army will consume a full third of its energies in an elaborate system of mystification. A modern army must either

A YOUNG WIDOW AT HER HUSBAND'S GRAVE

banish the war correspondent altogether or subject him to such restrictions of Censorship as to veto honest, accurate, and prompt criticism or record of operations.

The Bulgarian army had not the courage to refuse authorisation to the swarm of journalists which descended upon its headquarters. Editors had argued it out that the small Balkan States, anxious to have a " good press " in Europe, would give correspondents a good show. But the Bulgarian authorities, anxious as they were to conciliate foreign public opinion, dared not allow a free run to the newspaper representatives. Apart from the considerations I have mentioned, which must govern any modern war, there were special reasons why the Bulgarians should be nervous of observation. They were waging war on " forlorn hope " lines with the slenderest resources, with the knowledge that officers and men—especially transport officers—had to do almost the impossible to win through. Further, they had the knowledge that in some cases the correspondents were representing the newspapers (and the Governments, for newspapers and cabinets often work hand in hand on the Continent) of nations which were at the very moment threatening mobilisation against the Balkan States. To have specially excepted Roumanian, Austrian, and German press representatives from permission to see operations would have been impossible. The method was adopted of authorising as many press correspondents as cared to apply, then carefully pocketing them where they could see nothing, and instituting such a rigorous Censorship as to guard effectively against any important facts, gleaned indirectly, leaking out. A few managed to earn enough of the Bulgarian confidence to be allowed to go through to the front and see things. But, even then, the Censorship and the monopoly of the telegraph line for military messages prevented them from despatching anything.

Some of the correspondents—one in particular —overcame a secretive military system and a harsh Censorship by the use of a skilled imagination and of a friendly telegraph line outside the area of Censorship. At the staff headquarters at Stara Zagora during the early days of the campaign, when we were all straining at the leash to get to the front, waiting and fussing, he was working, reconstructing the operations with maps and a fine imagination, and never allowing his

A WAR CORRESPONDENT'S TRIALS 107

paper to want for news. I think that he was quite prepared to have taken pupils for his new school of war correspondents. Often he would come to me for a yarn—in halting French on both sides—and would explain the campaign as it was being carried on. One eloquent gesture he habitually had—a sweeping motion which brought his arms together as though they were gathering up a bundle of spears, then the hands would meet in an expressive squeeze. " It is that," he said, " it is Napoleonic."

Probably the Censor at this stage did not interfere much with his activities, content enough to allow fanciful descriptions of Napoleonic strategy to go to the outer world. But, in my experience, facts, if one ascertained something independently, were not treated kindly.

" Why not ? " I asked the Censor vexedly about one message he had stopped. " It is true."

" Yes, that is the trouble," he said—the nearest approach to a joke I ever got out of a Bulgarian, for they are a sober, God-fearing, and humour-fearing race.

The idea of the Bulgarian Censorship in regard to the privileges and duties of the war correspondent was further illustrated to me on another occasion, when a harmless map of a past phase of the campaign was stopped.

"Then what am I to send?" I asked.

"There are the bulletins," he said.

"Yes, the bulletins which are just your bald official account of week-old happenings which are sent to every news-agency in Europe before we see them!"

"But you are a war correspondent. You can add to them in your own language."

Remembering that conversation, I suspect that at first the Bulgarian Censorship did not object to fairy tales passing over the wires, though the way was blocked for exact observation. An enterprising story-maker had not very serious difficulties at the outset. Afterwards there was a change, and even the writer of fairy stories had to work outside the range of the Censor.

We were all allowed down to Mustapha Pasha, and considered that that was a big step to the front. "For two days or so," we were told, it would be our duty to wait patiently within the town (the battle-ground around Adrianople was about twelve miles distant). Some waited there two months and saw no real operations. The Censorship at Mustapha Pasha was so strict that all private letters had to be submitted, and if they were in English the English Censor insisted that they should be read to him aloud; and he re-read them, again aloud, to see if he had fully grasped their significance. Then they could go if they contained no military information and did not mention guns, oxen, soldiers, roads, mud, dirt, or other tabooed subjects. An amusing " rag " was tried on the Censor there. A sorely tried correspondent wrote a letter of extreme warmth to an imaginary sweetheart. This began " Ducksie Darling," and continued in the same strain for two pages. He waited until there was a full house—the Censors had no private office, but did their censoring in a large room which was open to all the correspondents—and then submitted his ardent outburst. Other pressmen did not see the joke at first, and began to sidle out of the room as, like a stream of warm treacle, the love-letter flowed on. But they came back.

" ' Ducksie Darling,' " began the writer, " that, you know, is not a military term. It is a phrase of endearment used in England.—' A thousand, thousand kisses '—that has nothing to do with the disposition of troops." So he went through to the honeyed end, the Censor blushing and furious, the audience hilarious.

The Mustapha Pasha Censorship would not allow ox-wagons or reservists to be mentioned, nor officers' names. The Censorship objected, too, for a long time to any mention of the all-pervading mud which was the chief item of interest in the town's life. Yet you might have lost an army division in some of the puddles. (But stop, I am lapsing into the picturesque ways of the new school of correspondents. Actually you could not have lost more than a regiment in the largest mud-puddle.)

Let the position be frankly faced, that if one is with an army in modern warfare, common sense prohibits the authorities from allowing you to see anything, and suggests the further precautions of a strict Censorship and a general hold-up of wires until their military value (and therefore their " news " value) has passed. If your paper wants picturesque stories hot off the grill it is much better not to be with the army (which means, in effect, in the rear of the army), but to write about its deeds from outside the radius of the Censorship.

Perhaps, though, your paper has old-fashioned

prejudices in favour of veracity and will be annoyed if your imagination leads you too palpably astray? In that case do not venture to be a war correspondent at all. If you do not invent you will send nothing of value. If you invent you will be reprimanded.

Let me give my personal record of " getting to the front " and the net result of the trouble and the expense. I went down to Mustapha Pasha with the great body of war correspondents, and soon recognised that there was no hope of useful work there. The attacking army was at a standstill and a long, wearisome siege—its operations strictly guarded from inspection—was in prospect. I decided to get back to staff headquarters (then at Stara Zagora), and just managed to catch the staff before it moved on to Kirk Kilisse. By threatening to return to London at once I got a promise of leave to join the Third Army and to " see some fighting."

The promise anticipated the actual granting of leave by two days. It would be tedious to record all the little and big difficulties that were then encountered through the reluctance of the military authorities to allow one to get transport or help of any kind. But four days later I was marching out of Mustapha Pasha on the way to Kirk Kilisse by way of Adrianople, a bullock-wagon carrying my baggage, an interpreter trundling my bicycle, I riding a small pony. The interpreter was gloomy and disinclined to face the hardships and dangers (mostly fancied) of the journey. Beside the driver (a Macedonian) marched a soldier with fixed bayonet. Persuasion was necessary to force the driver to undertake the journey, and a friendly transport officer had, with more or less legality, put at my command this means of argument. A mile outside Mustapha Pasha the soldier turned back, and I was left to coax my unwilling helpers on a four days' journey across a war-stricken country-side, swept of all supplies, infested with savage dogs (fortunately well fed by the harvest of the battlefields), liable to ravage by roving bands.

That night I gave the Macedonian driver some jam and some meat to eke out his bread and cheese.

"That is better than having a bayonet poked into your inside," I said, by pantomime. He understood, grinned, and gave no great trouble thereafter, though he was always in a state of

GIPSIES

A WAR CORRESPONDENT'S TRIALS   113

pitiable funk when I left the wagon to take a trip within the lines of the besieging forces.

So to Kirk Kilisse. There I got to General Savoff himself and won not only leave, but a letter of aid to go down to the Third Army at the lines of Chatalja. But by then what must be the final battle of the war was imminent. Every hour of delay was dangerous. To go by cart meant a journey of several days. A military train was available part of the way if I were content to drop interpreter, horse, and baggage and travel with a soldier's load.

That decision was easy enough at the moment —though I sometimes regretted it afterwards when the only pair of riding-breeches I had with me gave out at the knees, and I had to walk the earth ragged—and by train I got to Tchorlu. There a friendly artillery officer helped me to get a cart (springless) and two fast horses. He insisted also on giving me as a patrol, a single Bulgarian soldier, with 200 rounds of ammunition, as Bashi-Bazouks were ranging the country. I objected that I had a revolver, and there was the driver, a Greek. "He would run away," said the officer pleasantly, and the patrol was taken.

It was an unnecessary precaution, though the presence of the soldier was comforting as we entered Silivri at night, the outskirts of the town deserted, the chattering of the driver's teeth audible over the clamour of the cart, the gutted houses ideal refuges for prowling bands. From Silivri to Chatalja there was again no appearance of Bashi-Bazouks. But thought of another danger obtruded as we came near the lines and encountered men from the Bulgarian army suffering from the choleraic dysentery which had then begun its ravages. To one dying soldier by the roadside I gave brandy; and then had to leave him with his mates, who were trying to get him to a hospital. They were sorely puzzled by his cries, his pitiful grimaces. Wounds they knew, and the pain of them they despised. They could not comprehend this disease which took away all the manhood of a stoic peasant, and made him weak in spirit as an ailing child.

From Chatalja, the right flank of the Bulgarian position, I passed along the front to Ermenikioi ("the village of Armenians"), passing the night at Arjenli, near the centre and the headquarters of the ammunition park. That night at Arjenli seemed to make a rough and sometimes perilous journey, which had extended over seven days, worth while.

Arjenli is perched on a high hill, to the west of Ermenikioi. It gave a view of all the Chatalja position—the range of hills stretching from the Black Sea to the Sea of Marmora, along which the Bulgarians were entrenched, and, beyond the invisible valley, the second range which held the Turkish defence. Over the Turkish lines, like a standard, shone in the clear sky a crescent moon, within its tip a bright star. It seemed an omen, an omen of good to the Turks. My Australian eye instinctively sought for the Southern Cross ranged against it in the sky in sign that the Christian standard held the Heavens too. I sought in vain in those northern latitudes, shivered a little and, as though arguing against a superstitious thought, said to myself: " But there is the Great Bear."

For by this time I had come to sympathise thoroughly with the Bulgarian army and its cause. The soldiers were such good fellows: their steadiness, their sense of justice, their kindness were so remarkable. Just an incident of the camp at Arjenli to illustrate this. It was on the Friday night of November 15, and on the morrow we expected the decisive battle of the war. At Arjenli (which was a little to the rear of the Bulgarian lines) was the ammunition park of the artillery, guarded by a small body of troops under Lieutenant-Colonel Tchobanoff. Coming towards the front from Tchorlu, the fall of night and the weariness of my horses had compelled me to halt at the village, and this officer and Dr. Neytchef gave me a warm welcome to their little Mess.

There are six members, and for all, to sleep and to eat, one room. Three are officers, three have no commissions. With this nation in arms that is not an objection to a common table. Discipline is strict, but officers and soldiers are men and brothers when out of the ranks. Social position does not govern military position. I found sometimes the University professor and the bank manager without commissions, the peasant proprietor an officer. The whole nation had poured out its manhood for the war, from farm, field, factory, shop, bank, university, and consulting-room.

Here at Arjenli on the eve of the decisive battle, I think over early incidents of the campaign. It is a curious fact that in all Bulgaria I have met but one man who was young enough and well enough to fight and who had not enlisted. He had become an American subject, I believe, and so could not be compelled to serve. In America he had learned to be an "International Socialist," and so he did not volunteer. I believe he was unique. With half the population of London, Bulgaria had put 350,000 trained men under arms.

We eat our simple meal of goat's flesh stewed with rice. Then, smoking cigarettes made of the tobacco of the district, Colonel Tchobanoff and I talk over the position as well as my bad French will allow. He is serene and cheerful. His chief care is to impress upon me the fact that in making war the Bulgarians had not been influenced by dynastic considerations nor by military ambition. It was a war dictated not by a Court circle or a military clique, but by the irresistible wish of the people.

Whilst we were talking the sound of a rifle shot came up from the village. A junior officer was sent out to make inquiries. Soon he returned with two soldiers leading between them a Turkish prisoner.

I learn the facts. The Turk had tried to rush

past a sentry standing guard over the ammunition park. The sentry had fired, had not hit the man, but had grappled with him afterwards and taken him prisoner.

I nerved myself to see the Turk shot out of hand. The rules of war warranted it. He had tried to rush a sentry on guard over an important military station. But the Bulgarian officers decided to hear his story, and a kind of informal court-martial was constituted. The proceedings, which were in Turkish, were translated to me, as I was acting in a way as friend of the accused to " see fair play."

The Turk's story was clear enough. He had lived in Arjenli all his life and was not a soldier. When the Turkish army had evacuated the district he had not left with them, but had stayed in his old village. That night he had gone out of his hut to the village well. Returning, a sentry had challenged him, and he had become frightened and tried to run away.

It was clear that the man was telling the truth. The Bulgarians believed him, and let him go with a warning. This showed justice and courage, and a good " nerve " too. In some armies, I suspect, the Turk would have been shot, or hanged first and left to explain afterwards, if he could. And this was among the Bulgarians, who some insist are a bloodthirsty, cut-throat race, with no sense of justice or of mercy!

CHAPTER VIII

INCIDENTS OF BULGARIAN CHARACTER

SOME further incidents of Bulgarian life gleaned during war-time will illustrate the national characteristics of the people.

Peter was a secretary-servant whom I engaged at Sofia to accompany me to the front because he could speak English, a language he had learned at the Robert (American) College in Constantinople, where he was educated. Peter was to be partly a secretary, partly a servant. He was to interpret for me, translate Bulgarian papers and documents, also to cook and to carry if need be. He was destined to be a lawyer, and was the son of a small trader.

Peter was interesting as illustrating the transition stage between the Bulgarian peasant (for whom I have the heartiest admiration) and the Bulgarian statesman, diplomat, " personage "

A PEASANT OF THE TSARIBROD DISTRICT

INCIDENTS OF BULGARIAN CHARACTER

(for whom I have not—generally speaking and with particular exceptions—nearly so much admiration). He had not lost the peasant virtues. He was loyal, plucky, patriotic. But he had lost the good health and the practical knowledge of life of the peasant stock from which he sprang.

The Bulgarian on the land lives a laborious life, bread and cheese his usual sole food, with a little meat as a rare treat, and a glass of vodka as his indulgence for Sundays and feast days only. Marrying early he is astonishingly fecund. Transfer him to town life and he soon shows a weakening in physical fibre. The streets sap away his field-bred health. A more elaborate diet attacks the soundness of his almost bovine digestion. There is no greater contrast between the Bulgarian peasant on the land, physically the healthiest type one could imagine, and the Bulgarian town resident, who has not yet learned to adapt himself to the conditions of closely hived life and shows a marked susceptibility to dyspepsia, phthisis, and neurasthenia. The Bulgarian peasant has the nerves, the digestion of an ox. The Bulgarian town-dweller, the son or grandson of that peasant, might pass often for the tired-out progeny of many generations of city workers.

Peter could not serve in the army because his lungs were affected. That was why he was available as my secretary-servant. Peter was, as regards any practical knowledge of life, the most pathetically useless young man one could imagine. He could make coffee, after the Turkish fashion, and had equipped himself for a long campaign with a most elaborate coffee machine, all glass and gimcrackery, which of course did not survive one day's travel. But he had not brought food nor cooking pots nor knife nor fork nor spoon: no blankets had he, and no change of clothing— just the coffee-pot, a picture of a saint, and an out-of-date book of Bulgarian statistics, which he solemnly presented to me, with his name affectionately inscribed on the fly-leaf. I dared not throw it away, and so had to carry its useless bulk about with me until Peter and I parted. In addition to his lack of equipment, Peter could not roll a rug, make a bed, or fend for himself in any way.

The Bulgarian peasant in his life on the land is on the whole a very clever chap as regards the practical things of existence. During the campaign I noticed how he made himself very comfortable. Whenever he was stationed as a guard for a railway bridge or in any other semi-permanent post, he half-dug, half-thatched himself an excellent shelter. He made use for food supplies of every scrap of eatable stuff that came his way, and could do wonders in the manipulation and repair of an ox-cart. But clearly these simple skills do not survive town life. Peter was only one example of many that I encountered. The problem that troubles Bulgaria to-day and will trouble her for some time to come is that of finding from her almost exclusively peasant population enough statesmen, lawyers, priests, teachers, leaders generally who will have substituted for peasant virtues and peasant abilities the *savoir faire* of the cultivated European. They show a tendency to lose the one before they gain the other.

My life with Peter was brief. He was such a good fellow that I was quite willing to retain him, even though I had to be the servant really, and his services were only useful as interpreter. But his health improved. Possibly the better food and the open-air regime that I insisted upon were responsible. Peter became healthy enough to do something for the army and, of course, he went away to do that something. Though he had become a good deal devoted to me his chief devotion was to his country. I honoured him for deserting me.

Incidents of the mobilisation of the troops showed this strong and general patriotic ardour. At the call this trained nation was in arms in a day. The citizen soldiers hurried to the depôts for their arms and uniforms. In one district the rumour that mobilisation had been authorised was bruited abroad a day before the actual issue of the orders, and the depôt was besieged by the peasants who had rushed in from their farms. The officer in charge could not give out the rifles, so the men lit fires, got food from the neighbours, and camped around the depôt until they were armed. Some navvies received their mobilisation orders on returning to their camp after ten hours' work at railway-building. They had supper and marched through the night to their respective headquarters. For one soldier, the march was twenty-four miles. The railway carriages were not adequate to bring all the men to their assigned centres. Some rode on the steps, on the roofs of carriages, on the buffers even.

At Stara Zagora I noted a mother of the people who had come to see some Turkish prisoners just brought in from Mustapha Pasha. To one she gave a cake. "They are hungry," she said. This woman had five men at the war, her four sons in the fighting-line, her husband under arms guarding a line of communication. She had sent them proudly. It was the boast of the Bulgarian women that not a tear was shed at the going away of the soldiers.

At a little village outside Kirk Kilisse a young civil servant, an official of the Foreign Office, spoke of the war whilst we ate a dish of cheese and eggs. " It is a war," he said, " of the peasants and the intellectuals. It is not a war made by the politicians or the soldiers of the staff. That would be impossible. In our nation every soldier is a citizen and every citizen a soldier. There could not be a war, unless it were a war desired by the people. In my office it was with rage that some of the clerks heard that they must stay at Sofia, and not go to the front. We were all eager to take arms."

At Nova Zagora, travelling by a troop train carrying reserves to the front, I crossed a train bringing wounded from the battlefields. For some hours both trains were delayed. The men going to the front were decorated with flowers as though going to a feast. They filled the waiting time by dancing to the music of the national bagpipes, and there joined in the dance such of the wounded as could stand on their feet.

At Mustapha Pasha I arrived one night from Stara Zagora with a great body of correspondents. With me I had brought about a week's supply of food, leaving other supplies with my heavy baggage. But on the train journey, taking up a full day, this supply disappeared. No one else seemed to have food supplies handy, and I fed all I could, including a Bulgarian bishop (who showed his gratitude afterwards by " cutting me dead " when it was in his power to do me a slight favour). When we reached Mustapha Pasha it was to find no hotels, lodging-houses, cafés, or stores. All the food supplies had been requisitioned by the Bulgarian military authorities. There was plenty of food in the town but none could be bought. I tried to get a loaf of bread from a military bakery, offering to the soldier in charge up to five francs for a loaf. He was sturdily proof against bribes. But subsequently I was given a loaf for nothing on the ground that I was " in distress "; as indeed I was, though with £100 in my pocket.

INCIDENTS OF BULGARIAN CHARACTER 127

Between Silivri and Ermenikioi, travelling with a fine equipment for the time being—a cart and two good horses and a full supply of food, purchased at Tchorlu and Silivri—I was eating lunch by the roadside when four Bulgarian soldiers came up and with signs told me that they were starving, and asked for food. They had become separated from their regiment and, I gathered, had had no food for two days. They were armed with rifles and bayonets and could have taken from me all they needed if they had wished. But that thought did not seem to have entered their heads. I gave them a meal and a little bread and cheese to see them on their way. One of these poor peasant soldiers fumbled in his purse and brought out some coppers, wishing to pay for what he had had.

Repeatedly in my travels I would come at nightfall to some little vedette outpost and be made welcome of the officers' Mess. That meant sharing their meal, whatever it was,—a very poor one sometimes. After the main dish I would bring out dates and biscuits, of which I had a small store, to find usually that the Bulgarian officers would refuse to trench upon my supplies, as I was going forward " to the front " and would need them. That was not the attitude of savages but of gentlemen.

These and a score of similar incidents showed me the Bulgarian national character as kind, honest, patient, courageous. They made it impossible for me to believe that by nature these people are invariably cruel, rapacious, murderous. That in cases of Balkan massacres and outrages the Bulgarian people have not been always the victims, and have not been always blameless, I know. It is impossible to shut one's eyes to the fact that something survives of the traditions of cruelty and reprisal existing in the Balkans of the Middle Ages. In this Balkan peninsula there is always a smell of blood in the nostrils, a mist of blood in the eyes. The Bulgarians have taken their part in many incidents which seem to deny the existence of Christian civilisation.

But I speak of the people as I found them, and I came away from the Balkans confident that my life and property would always be safe with Bulgarian peasants, provided that I made no movement to begin trouble. I came away, too, with a high idea of their essential soundness as a nation and their certainty of a great future. Allowances have to be made for the hostility of

THE RATCHENITZA, THE NATIONAL DANCE OF BULGARIA

circumstances. As is insisted by the Bulgarians, when the little nation started to restore its old home life, everything had to be replaced. "It was not only the political conditions which had altered, but social life itself. At a moment's notice, and practically out of nothing, a new administration had to be organised and the diverse organs of the national life to be improvised. Hardly anything valuable of the preceding regime could be utilised. In this connection, it is interesting to observe the different fortunes of a conquered province. When a province which had formed part of a civilised country passes to a nation equally civilised, one may say that in many respects the change is an unimportant one, because in such a case the conqueror retains almost all the institutions, the only difference being that in the future they work in the name of the new sovereign authority. The political condition of such a province is the only thing which is affected, the administrative and judicial system and the wealth continuing as before. On the other hand, if one attempted to form a modern state out of a country which has been devastated for centuries, or if one tried to transform a Turkish province into a country after the pattern of the European States, every step would be strewn with obstacles, and there would be nothing of the former state of things that could be utilised. In such a case, the only thing to be done would be to borrow from other nations the experience which they have accumulated during their long efforts, and to transplant it into the desolated land. This is practically what happened in Bulgaria, and it is only by taking into account the exceptionally difficult conditions in which the Principality found itself on the morrow of its liberation that one will be able to appreciate the efforts displayed and the result obtained."

In one particular there is to a British observer a marked failing in the Bulgarian character : the Bulgars are very nervous to "keep up appearances" and that makes them appear snobbish and deceitful at times. They are ashamed of poverty, a little ashamed, too, of their natural manners. Always they wish to put the best face on things before the world. If a Bulgarian understood that you recognised any crudeness anywhere he liked to pretend that it was not a usual thing but a temporary circumstance due to the war. I got quite tired of hearing " *La guerre comme la guerre* " murmured to me by apologetic

Bulgarians wanting to pretend that under normal circumstances his countrymen always had the best of table silver and napery.

One incident (which left nothing but amiable memories) of a day's march north of Adrianople I can recall illustrating this desire to keep up appearances. After an anxious day I had got to a Bulgarian camp, was welcomed by an officer and brought around to a little hut where the mess was established. My new-made friend knocked at the door and explained things in Bulgarian. I heard a scuffle and could not help seeing through the window two young officers who were comfortably enjoying supper with their coats off rushing to get into full uniform. Until they were dressed properly there was no admittance to the stranger. That showed on the whole a good feeling of pride: but sometimes Bulgarian sensitiveness to criticism and desire to appear grand was a little trying. I suppose, however, it is natural in a "new" people.

In most things, however, the Bulgarian is intensely practical. That sturdy panegyrist of the Bulgars, Mr. Noel Buxton, M.P., insists upon this practicality even when its effects were notably absent :

"The Bulgarian mind," he writes, "is practical. It is no doubt still debated, among European military experts, whether the army succeeded through a well-organised transport or in spite of the want of it. The foreign Red Cross contingents at the front were inclined to the latter view. Judged by English or by German standards, the system, or want of system, employed led them to suppose that success came from 'muddling through.' They found that nothing was prepared for their arrival, and no classification of the wounded carried out. But it may be doubted whether the Bulgarian mind does not include some elements of a quality which is really higher than statistical efficiency."

It calls for a more affectionate eye towards the Bulgar people than I possess to be blind to the fact that in their medical and sanitary arrangements for the campaign against the Turks they were woefully deficient. The excuse of ignorance is the only one that will serve. The only alternative to that would be a complete recklessness for life. In the Bulgarian camps sanitary precautions were absolutely lacking, and on the battlefields the provision for dealing with the wounded was shockingly inadequate. When I came back from Chatalja to Kirk Kilisse, King Ferdinand sent his private secretary for me as an independent witness of the state of things at the front. I took the occasion to acquaint His Majesty frankly with the ghastly consequences that had followed from the absence of all precautions to ensure a wholesome water supply, from the neglect of latrine regulations in the camps and other failures in the medical and sanitary service. I had no reason to feel that my frankness was resented, and I believe that (too late in the day) an effort at reform was made. Certainly since then there has been reform, and if Bulgaria should unhappily have to enter upon another campaign probably the medical and sanitary services will be brought to a high pitch of organisation.

Yes, the Bulgarian is very practical in mind but he has suffered, and has yet to suffer again perhaps, from lack of experience to instruct his practical mind. If the national pride would allow of it, an excellent thing for Bulgaria would be to import half a dozen skilled officials from, say, England and France to nurse her departments through the stage of infancy. The nation has plenty of natural genius but makes mistakes through inexperience.

CHAPTER IX

THE TRAGEDY OF 1914

WHEN the war between the Balkan States and the Turkish Empire was brought to a close for the time being by an armistice signed on the battlefield of Chatalja, to which Bulgaria, Servia, and Turkey were parties, and by the summoning of the Conference of London, to which Greece also was a party, the prospects for Bulgaria's future were singularly bright. As a power in the Balkans Turkey had ceased to exist. She had been driven out of all Albania, Macedonia, Epirus, and Thrace, except that beleaguered garrisons held the fortresses of Scutari, Janina, and Adrianople and the Dardanelles forts, whilst behind the lines of Chatalja a small area of Turkish territory remained under the Crescent. The area held by the Bulgarian armies was greater at this time than the territory assigned to her by the Treaty of San Stefano, and promised to be extended as the result of the peace negotiations. In the war which had just been waged the exploits of Bulgarian arms had attracted the widest attention in Europe. Public opinion in most of the capitals of the world assigned the future hegemony of the Balkan Peninsula to the Bulgarian nation. But all this fair-seeming prospect was the prelude to one of the greatest national tragedies in history.

I cannot better preface a relation of the facts of that tragedy than by giving a summary of the position early in 1914, as it was given anonymously by a noted Bulgarian diplomat to the *National Review*. He wrote:

> It is too late for pretending that all is well with the Balkan League. Even in official quarters, where pessimism is generally discouraged, it is no longer denied that relations between the Allies have reached a critical stage. . . . It would form a sad epilogue to a noble story if what began as a crusade of liberation were to end in fratricidal strife. . . . Nominally, the quarrel turns on the interpretation of treaties and their bearing on the situation created by the war. But underneath all these arguments there lurk preoccupations far transcending the scope of written or oral agreements. The question at stake is nothing less than the future balance of power in the Balkans. The map of the Balkans has

been transformed beyond recognition, and Turkey has practically ceased to exist as a European power; but those who expected it to inaugurate an era of tranquillity have been disappointed. The failure of the war as an instrument of pacification is largely due to the very magnitude of its military success. Had the victories of the Allies been less decisive, conditions might have arisen more favourable to the cause of Balkan union. The sudden collapse of Turkey left a void which has upset the entire scheme of things existing. . . .

The passions which the war has engendered are only partly due to lust for territorial aggrandisement. Mere thirst after conquest would have never produced such perversions of moral sense had it not been backed by the sentiment of fear and jealousy. This is clearly proved by the fact that feelings have reached their highest point of intensity where this latter element loomed largest. The Bulgarians have exhibited a degree of self-control which is in marked contrast with the conduct of other Allies. This equanimity is the more surprising in view of the fact that the position of Bulgaria is wellnigh desperate. For months past, the brunt of the war has fallen almost entirely on her. On every side she is surrounded by an atmosphere of open hostility. By threats of invasion, Roumania has wrung from her a ransom for the Balkan victories, while in Macedonia her allies are preparing to dispute her lawful share and have massed against her their whole armies. So long as peace with Turkey is not signed she must remain immobilised in front of Chatalja and Bulair. For a parallel case one must go back to the dark hours of Prussia during the Seven Years' War. But in the midst of all these difficulties Bulgaria has kept a cool head, whereas public opinion in Servia and Greece has parted company with

A BAGPIPER

all reason. It is not indifference to the issues at stake which explains this placid demeanour. When the proper time arrives, the Bulgarians will be found tough bargainers and determined to claim their full due. They know, however, that the position of their country as prime factor in the Balkans cannot be seriously affected by the results of the allotment. Even before the war, the supremacy of Bulgaria was hardly questioned, and the formation of the Balkan League would have been impossible but for this acquiescence in her right to leadership. With the disappearance of Turkey, this predominance is bound to be further accentuated and henceforth will have to be reckoned with as a political axiom.

The reasons which have enabled Bulgaria to envisage the future with tranquillity are for her allies a source of uneasiness. Servia and Greece have long watched the rapid and uninterrupted progress of their pushful neighbour with mixed feelings of fear and envy. Her seniors in point of time, they have been outdistanced in the race for Balkan hegemony. In 1885 Servia made a desperate attempt at grappling with the problem, but had no reason to be satisfied with the results. The doctrine of Balkan equilibrium was buried at Slivnitza, and since then Servia has had to rest contented with a secondary place. But the galling memory of defeat had never died out and probably plays in the present anti-Bulgarian agitation a larger part than most Servians realise or would care to admit.

Antagonism between Greeks and Bulgarians is a legacy of the past. Their history is a long record of ceaseless struggle. When they could no longer war as freemen, the feud was transferred to ecclesiastical ground and there continued under the mocking eye of their new masters. Since their restoration to independent life, they have not been able to revert to the old tradition owing to Turkey's presence as buffer state. This involuntary truce, however, has not turned hatred into love. They are once more to have a common frontier and will thus be brought in direct contact.

. . . The war has widened the gulf between these races by adding to the old stock of animosities a fresh supply of military jealousies. It has let loose over the entire Peninsula a flood of vanity which has upset the balance of a good many heads. A year ago, no sane Servian would have dreamed of pitting his country against Bulgaria, and this recognition of inferiority stood for peace. Now, every Servian officer is convinced that the result of such a trial of forces would be favourable to Servia, just as he is persuaded that the issues of the war with Turkey have been decided mainly by Servian valour. . . .

If this is the way in which Servians are wearing their laurels, it can be imagined what the effect of recent events has been on impressionable Greece. To the trepidation with which the war was entered has succeeded the feeling of boundless self-reliance. All sense of reality and proportion has been banished, and there is no exploit which seems beyond the reach of Greek effort.

The outbreak of a fresh Balkan war would, in the present circumstances, prove little short of a world-wide calamity. Should, however, Europe succeed in localising such a conflict, its miseries will, to a certain extent, be compensated by one very important advantage. A trial of forces between the various Balkan competitors will clear the atmosphere and settle in the only efficacious way the sore problem of Balkan hegemony, which is at the bottom of Balkan unrest. It will fix for a long term of years the respective positions of the parties. Just as the Servo-Bulgarian War in 1885 proved a blessing in disguise, so this time also the arbitrament of the sword might create conditions more favourable to the political stability of the Peninsula. And this will be a gain not only to the Balkan nations, but to the whole of Europe.

The last thing of which that Bulgarian writer dreamt was the actual result of the fresh Balkan war, which did break out and which ended in the humiliation of Bulgaria. He contemplated the necessity of palliating to European minds the enormity of a fratricidal war between allies who had sanctioned their war against Turkey as a struggle of the Cross against the Crescent; but he had no idea that there was the barest possibility that Bulgaria would have to suffer complete defeat instead of explaining victory.

The Conference of London which endeavoured to arrange a peace after the first phase of the Balkan war met first in December 1913. I watched closely its deliberations, had several friends among the delegates, and was in a position to see at close hand the play of jealousies and ambitions which made its work futile. From the first the very desperation of Turkey raised a difficulty to quick peace negotiations. She had lost so much as to be practically bankrupt, and was in the position of a reckless man with no more possible losses to suffer, anxious by any expedient to postpone the day of payment in the hope that something would turn up in his favour. That anything should turn up seemed in reason impossible, but Oriental fatalism despises reason; and in this case Oriental fatalism was right judged by the final event.

The sessions of the London Conference found a vividly contrasting setting in London. (In Constantinople the meetings would have had an appropriate stage.) It was a contest of Oriental against semi-Oriental diplomacy; and staid British officials, who had duties in connection with the Conference, lived for weeks in an atmosphere of bewilderment, wondering if they were still in the twentieth century or had wandered back to the Bagdad of the Middle Ages.

The first effort of the Turkish delegates was to gain time. On any point that arose they wanted instructions from their government and pressed for an adjournment. When, after a few days, the Conference assembled again, the instructions had not arrived, and there was need for another adjournment. At the next meeting the in-

THE TRAGEDY OF 1914 141

structions had arrived; but they were written so illegibly that they could not be deciphered, and so there was another adjournment. (This illegible despatches excuse had not even the merit of being novel—it was used many years before in an Egyptian negotiation.) To the desperate attempts of the Turks to waste time the diplomats of the Balkan States replied with but little patience or suavity. They did not recognise fully that they were present at a deathbed, and that the patient had some excuse for taking an unconscionable time in dying. Their patience was not increased by the knowledge of the fact that the time secured by these evasive excuses was being used in desperate attempts to sow dissensions among the allies and to beat up support in some European capital for the forlorn Turkish Empire.

It was over the question of the cession of Adrianople to Bulgaria that the chief trouble arose, and the Turkish delegates made a great point of the fact that at Adrianople was the parent mosque of Islam in Europe and the burial-place of the first Sultans. This plea for their holy places aroused some sympathy in Europe. I suggested to Dr. Daneff, the chief Bulgarian delegate to the Conference, that he should allow me to publish that Bulgaria would allow the Turks to retain the holy places in Adrianople as an extra-territorial area under the control of the Moslem Caliph. Dr. Daneff liked the proposal, but at first would only allow it to go out as an unofficial hint that probably Bulgaria would consent to such an arrangement. Then, finding that the concession was popular, he fathered it directly, and it was made one of the terms of peace which the Powers tried to force upon Turkey.

Peace seemed assured when finally the Turkish Porte agreed, under pressure from the Powers, to a Treaty of Peace, which left to Turkey on the European mainland only the territory lying south and east from a line drawn between Media, on the Black Sea, to Rodosto on the Sea of Marmora. But a revolution in Turkey upset this arrangement, and the Peace Conference was broken up and the war resumed.

In this second phase of the Balkan war against Turkey (1914), the efforts of the Balkan League were practically confined to attacks upon the fortresses still held by the Turks in the conquered territories. Scutari, Janina, Adrianople fell after fierce battles. The revolution clearly had done nothing to restore the military strength of the Turks. Now another effort was made to end the war, and the Peace Conference resumed its sessions in London.

Whilst during the 1913 session all the delay had been caused by Turkey, now Turkey shared the willingness of Bulgaria to sign a peace on terms dictated by the Powers, which left to Turkey the territory behind the Midia-Rodosto line, and reserved for a European decision the fate of the Aegean Islands and the boundaries of an independent state of Albania which was to be set up. But both Servia and Greece were reluctant now to assent to such peace conditions. Both felt a grievance about the creation of an independent Albania which deprived them of a great stretch of territory on the Adriatic which they had hoped to share. Both felt that yet another war was necessary to settle issues as to the division of the spoil with Bulgaria.

To the delays for which Servia and Greece were responsible there was an added complication arising from the attitude of Roumania. That kingdom—which had taken no active part in the late war, but which had secretly nursed a boundary grievance against Bulgaria dating back from the War of Liberation, when Russia robbed Roumania of Bessarabia and proposed to pay her with Bulgarian territory without actually doing so—now announced that she must be a party to any new Balkan settlement, and mobilised her forces to give accent to the demand she had been making for some time for a territorial concession from Bulgaria.

The diplomacy of Bulgaria under these difficult circumstances was deplorable. Her statesmen seemed bemused with the intoxication of Bulgarian military victories, and unable to forget the glowing calculations of the future Bulgarian Empire which they had made during the course of the war. Those calculations I gathered from gossip with all classes in Bulgaria at different times, speaking not only with politicians but with bankers, trading people, and others. They concluded that the Turk was going to be driven out of Europe, at any rate, as far as Constantinople. They considered that Constantinople was too great a prize for the Bulgarian nation or for the Balkan States, and that Constantinople would be left as an international city to be governed by a commission of the Great Powers.

A YOUNG GIRL OF IRN

THE TRAGEDY OF 1914 145

Bulgaria was, then, to have of what had been Turkey-in-Europe, the province of Thrace, and a large part of Macedonia as far as the city of Salonica.

Salonica was desired very much by the Bulgarians, and also very much by the Greeks; and the decision in regard to Salonica before the war was that it would be best to make it a free Balkan city, governed by all the Balkan States in common, as a free port for all the Balkan States. The frontier of Greece was to extend to the north, and Greece was to be allowed all the Aegean Islands. The Servian frontier was to extend to the eastward and the southward, and what is now the autonomous province of Albania (the creation of which was insisted on by the Powers) was to be divided between Montenegro and Servia.

That division would have left the Bulgarians with the greatest spoil of the war. They would have had entry on to the Sea of Marmora; they would have controlled, perhaps, one side of the Dardanelles (but I believe they thought that the Dardanelles might also be left to a commission of the Powers). Now, with the clash of diplomacy, it was sternly necessary to curtail that ambition considerably, and to decide to seek a friend among the different rivals. Bulgarian diplomats could not be made to see that. They were firm with Turkey: wisely enough, for Turkey had no power left to wound or to help. But at the same time they refused to make any concessions either to Servia, to Greece, or to Roumania, all of whom were determined to have a share of the plunder which Bulgaria had assigned for herself. " A leonine partnership " as the lawyers call it, that is to say, a partnership in which one party takes the lion's share of the spoil, is a very satisfactory arrangement for the lion. But one wants to be sure before attempting to enforce leonine arrangements that one is the lion. Bulgaria blundered on into a position which left her exhausted army to face at once Greece, Servia, Montenegro, and Roumania.

That it was not necessary for her to get into that position I can say with some confidence. A more judicious handling of her relations with Servia would have kept the friendship of that kindred nation, and Montenegro would have followed Servia. The united Slav peoples of the Balkans would then have been strong enough to withstand any attempt to enforce unfair conditions by Roumania or Greece. But Bulgaria made no attempt to conciliate Servia. Between the two peoples there had existed before the war a very close treaty of alliance. This treaty had arranged for the division of the spoil of the war on a basis which had not foreseen that the European Powers would create an independent Albania; and Servia had not imagined that Turkey would be so weak, and that the booty in Thrace would have been so considerable. Bulgaria thus had more than was expected in one quarter, whilst Servia was bitterly disappointed in another direction. Friends, under the circumstances, would have struck another bargain. Bulgaria insisted upon the strict letter of the old bargain.

Servia was thus forced into the arms of Greece; reluctantly, I think. If she could have made a fair arrangement with Bulgaria she would have preferred that. But it seemed to be destined that Bulgaria should add another to the long list of her frustrated hopes.

The early part of 1914 saw the Balkans in the throes of a war which eclipsed in bitterness and bloodshed the campaign of 1913. Greece and Servia fought against Bulgaria, and Roumania marched down from the north towards the Bulgarian capital, her army unopposed because there was no means of opposing it. Stopping short of entering Sofia, Roumania took up the position of the chief Power in the Balkans and insisted upon dictating terms of peace. Those terms Bulgaria, perforce, accepted after her army had been defeated with terrible slaughter by the Servian and Grecian forces. She was forced to give up territory in all directions: to Roumania on the north; to Servia on the west; to Greece on the south. To crown her misfortunes, the Turks moved up against the prostrate country, recaptured, without an effort, Adrianople, which had been won with such terrible cost of Bulgarian blood, and also Kirk Kilisse. In the final result Bulgaria was left with but little net gain as the price of her enormous sacrifices of blood and of treasure. To the north she actually lost some of her old territory. From the Turk she secured a fragment of Thrace, and a part of Macedonia which gave her access to the Aegean Sea, but no decent port there, and no possibility of carrying out her grandiose scheme of canalising the River Maritza and making a Bulgarian Adrianople a port for trade. Further, she had the mortification of seeing all three of her rivals in the Balkans aggrandised, and Roumania left with the hegemony of the Peninsula.

Only a few months before, Mr. Noel Buxton had written the " Io triumphe " of the Bulgarian cause :

The blight that had lain on the Balkan lands was healed, the fog dispelled. Even the prestige of military despotism was gone like a pricked bubble. The tyranny that rested on delusion and not on power was vanished like an empty nightmare that fades when the sleeper wakes. The establishment of Europe's freedom was fulfilled ; the final step taken. A great and notable nation had obtained recognition through the war. Its persistence, its purpose, its deep reserve, now stood revealed, added to the world's stores of national character.

For centuries the Bulgarian refused to compromise with the Turk. Other nations sought to lighten the weight of the yoke by taking service with the tyrant or bowing the head. The maxim, " The sword never strikes when the head is bowed," undermined the soul of other nations, never of this. Influence and wealth went to others ; all seemed lost by the policy of defiance. Bulgarians would not balance advantages. A kind of faith made them ready to pay even death for ultimate gain. The spirit wins at last : and the indomitable spirit of the Bulgars has come by its just reward.

Three months after that the Turk was back in Thrace, and the national life of Bulgaria had touched its lowest point since the war of Liberation, with only her justified hope in the future as a consolation.

CHAPTER X

SOME FACTS FOR THE TOURIST AND THE ECONOMIST

BULGARIA is in the main tableau or plain land sheltered by lofty mountains. On the north it is bounded by the Danube until the town of Silistra is reached, when an artificial frontier cuts down from the river to the Black Sea coast. By the cession of territory to Roumania in 1914 this artificial frontier took a more southerly course, and reaches now to a point just north of Varna. The coast of the Black Sea bounds Bulgaria on the east, and she has there two ports, Varna and Burgas. On the south the frontier is now European Turkey as far west almost as the 24th parallel of latitude, and then the bordering territory is Greece. On the west the boundary is Servia. The Balkan Mountains and the Rhodope Mountains run roughly east and west:

the former almost in the centre of Bulgaria; the latter near to the Turkish border.

The valleys and plains of Bulgaria are watered by tributaries of the Danube, by tributaries of the Maritza and the Struma flowing into the Aegean Sea, and by some small streams flowing directly into the Black Sea. The soil of the plains and the tableland is generally good, and 70 per cent of it is suitable for cultivation. In the mountains there are a few small lakes and many deep gorges and noble peaks, offering to the traveller the attraction of scenery wilder than that of the Alps.

For the tourist with an autumn or a spring month to spare, I could imagine no more interesting journey than to cross on horseback or with an ox-wagon the Rhodopes or the Balkans. (In the summer such a tour would be less pleasant because of the heat of the plains and the prevalence of flies.) But in the autumn, of all seasons, the Balkan Peninsula has supreme charms. The climate then is perfect, usually fine, with warm clear days and cold nights. The atmosphere is full of light and colour. Sunset as seen from the lower foothills of the Balkans is a rare pageant of glowing colour. These foothills are covered with oak scrub, which with the first frosts of autumn puts on burning robes of red and gold. As the sun goes down to rest in the western sky, hung with banners of the same red and gold, the twilight steals up first as a pink radiance then as a deep purple glow. Light melts into light—softly, insensibly—the display in the sky and on the hill-sides gradually passing from one colour to another, until at last night and darkness come to end the long-drawn-out procession of colour.

These wild mountains abound in game which has been driven from the tamer parts of Europe. There are bears, wolves, jackals, wild boars, deer, chamois; and all kinds of birds, such as eagles, falcons, bustards, wild geese, pheasants, partridges, woodcock, snipe, and moorhen. For the sportsman the Balkan Peninsula is almost the only tract left in Europe offering really wild game. King Ferdinand, who recognises the tourist possibilities of his country, has lately encouraged the stocking of the Rhodope streams with trout, to offer another attraction to the visitor.

To King Ferdinand's initiative also is due in a great measure the movement to develop the

GUARDING THE FLOCKS AND HERDS

FACTS FOR THE TOURIST

spas of Bulgaria. The mountains abound in medicinal springs of various kinds. Some of the most important have been used in a primitive fashion since the Roman times, and under the Turkish rule. Recently, the mining section of the Ministry of Commerce and Agriculture has succeeded in developing the mineral springs at Sliven, Banki, Varshetz, and Meritchléri. Modern health-resorts have been built at Banki, Varshetz, Hissar, and Meritchléri. There are, all in all, more than 200 hot and mineral springs in Bulgaria in some eighty different places. In the department of Sofia there are twenty-three, the hottest of which is Dolnia Bania. The town of Sofia itself possesses very good hot springs. The municipality has almost completed the building of public baths which will cost £60,000.

Though it is far from the mind of the Bulgarian people to aim at making their country another playground for the west of Europe, there is no doubt at all but that in the future Bulgaria will attract, yearly, thousands of tourists—in the winter for snow-sports; in the spring and autumn for the scenery, the sport, the medicinal baths. At the present time there is practically no tourist traffic. Travellers wishing to explore early a new country may be confident of getting in the capital, Sofia, excellent hotel accommodation, and in the chief towns, such as Stara Zagora and Philippopolis, decent and clean accommodation. But to see Bulgaria properly it is necessary to take to horseback or wagon. At the capital it is possible to engage guides who speak English, and to hire horses or oxen for transport at an astonishingly cheap rate. The horse-carts of the country are springless and not too comfortable. The ox-wagons, also springless, are quite comfortable, as the oxen move along smoothly and without jerking. I have slept quite soundly in a Bulgarian ox-wagon as it crawled over roadless country at night.

Mainly an agricultural country, Bulgaria grows wheat, maize, barley, rye, oats, millet, spelt, rice (around Philippopolis), potatoes, grapes, tobacco, mulberries (there is a silk industry), and roses. This cultivation of roses for the production of attar of roses is an almost exclusively Bulgarian industry. Most of the genuine attar of roses produced in the world comes from Bulgaria. The production is a Government monopoly, and I believe that if care is taken to secure flasks of attar with the Government seal the purchaser may be sure of getting the genuine article. Otherwise, as likely as not, oil of geraniums is substituted for the attar of roses, or is used as an adulterant. The rose valleys are grouped around Stara Zagora, and a visit to the farms in the flowering season—late spring—should be an incident of a Balkan tour.

The exports of Bulgaria are chiefly cereals, and the imports manufactured goods of all kinds. But by a system of high Protection and bonuses efforts are being made to establish manufacturing industries in the country. The oldest Bulgarian industry is weaving, which has existed from ancient times as a home industry. The wool of the country was worked up into cloths, carpets, braids, serges, etc., which were in request throughout the Ottoman Empire. The most important weaving centres are Pirdop, Panaguiourichté, Karlovo, Sopot, Koprivchtitza, Klissoura, Kalofer, Gabrovo, Trevna, Sliven, Kotel, and Samokov. Under Turkish rule, these towns supplied cloth to the Imperial army. Bulgarian cloths were then held in esteem, and there was a demand for them in Greece and in Asia Minor. In 1880 some capitalists decided to start modern workshops.

The example was given by the towns of Gabrovo and Sliven, where there are now large factories, organised on modern principles. There are as many as twenty-six factories in other towns, among others, at Samokov and Kazanlik. Bulgaria holds the first place for weaving in the Balkan Peninsula. Lately, in addition to the making of woollens, cotton-spinning has been introduced, and there are several mills now working.

So pronounced has been the growth of industrialism in Bulgaria that labour legislation has been already found necessary. There are laws making regulations for the employment of apprentices, for the maximum number of hours in the working day, and the age of apprentices. The law of 1905 regulating the work of women and children lays down conditions for the employment of children under fifteen, and for women of all ages, occupied in factories, mines, quarries, workshops, and other industrial undertakings. Children of either sex who have not attained the age of twelve years must not be employed in factories, workshops, at pit-mouths, in quarries, or sewers. However, children under twelve, but in no case under ten, may be employed in certain undertakings. Children under fifteen and women under twenty-one cannot be employed in the subterranean parts of mines or quarries. The working day for children is limited to eight hours; night-work is forbidden to women, and to children under fifteen. On Sundays all industrial establishments must close.

In addition to these laws protecting workers there are laws protecting employers against foreign competition and granting them various bonuses. The general privileges, allowed to all industrial enterprises, are:

The use of water-power, without payment, where this is not on a private property;

Exemption from customs duties for such machines and parts of machines, tools, and accessories, needful for the installation of enterprise, as are not made in the Principality;

Exemption from customs duties for such building materials as are not found or made in the country;

Exemption from customs duties for raw material, when it is imported in order to be exported again, after having been worked up or finished off;

A free grant of land belonging to the State,

the province, or parish, for the installation of the factory;

Machinery, tools, coal, benzine, etc., for the factories are carried by the State railways at a rate 35 per cent below the lowest usual charge for those commodities. The law compels all public institutions to buy from native sources, even if native commodities should be as much as 15 per cent dearer than similar articles manufactured abroad.

Some industries have in addition special privileges allowed to them, such as exemptions from land taxation, monopoly privileges in certain districts, cheap coal from the State mines, etc. The Bulgarian national system aims at supplementing the agricultural resources of the country with industrial enterprises in every possible way. But agriculture is not neglected by the Government, and a special department exists to encourage improvement in cultivation and cattle-raising. This department has set up departmental councils, which distribute seeds every year. They make considerable grants to improve the breed of cattle. They also encourage progress in the farmers by organising competitions for poultry-rearing, fruit-growing, etc. Scholarships have

FACTS FOR THE TOURIST

been granted to a number of young men who wish to take up farming, so as to allow them to study methods in foreign agricultural schools.

Further, there is an agricultural bank which, curiously enough, dates back from the Turkish days. In 1863, Midhat Pasha, Governor of the Danubian Vilayet (*i.e.* Bulgaria), prepared a scheme for the creation of " urban " banks, which were intended to assist the rural population. The scheme having been approved by the Turkish Government, several of these banks were established. The peasants were allowed to repay in kind the loans which were advanced to them, the banks themselves selling the agricultural products. With the object of increasing the capital of the banks, a special tax was introduced obliging the farmers to hand every year to these institutions part of their produce in kind. These banks advanced money at 12 per cent interest—instead of up to 100 per cent, as the usurers generally did. The Turkish Government afterwards extended the reform to the whole Empire, and obliged the peasants to create similar banks in all the district centres. During the Russo-Turkish War several of these banks lost their funds, the functionaries of the Turkish Government having carried them away, as well as the securities and other property belonging to the banks' clients. After the war, the debtors refused to pay, and only part of the property of the banks was restored by means of the issue of new bonds. In 1894 the Bulgarian Government passed a law setting on a firm foundation these agricultural banks, and they have continued since to do good work for the peasant proprietors.

The Bulgarian is a great road-maker. He is always at work on new rail-roads and carriage roads. I travelled twice in 1913 between Mustapha Pasha and Kirk Kilisse (the country was then in Bulgarian occupation) with an interval of about a month between the journeys. During that month the Bulgarians had made a wonderful improvement in the road. Before, it had stopped short about a mile out of Mustapha Pasha and dwindled into a mere cart-track. After a month of Bulgarian work it had been so much improved as to make twenty-four hours' difference in the time of the journey. This improvement was carried through in time of war when there was much occupation for the national energy in more important directions. In other places I noted the Bulgarian's passion for a good road; and the

AN OLD STREET IN PHILIPPOPOLIS

FACTS FOR THE TOURIST 161

roads in his own country were excellent. The road-making instinct is a great proof of a stable sense of civilisation.

The Bulgarian railways are, with the quays at the ports, the property of the State, and are managed by a General Board of State Railways and Ports. There are over 3000 railway servants fourteen lines traversing the country east to west and north to south, and some seventy-two railway stations. Both Varna and Bourgas are connected by railway with the main lines. The lines have been constructed very cheaply (about £7500 a mile) considering the nature of the country which they traverse. They may be said to be profitable to the State since they return about $2\frac{1}{2}$ per cent interest on their cost of construction, despite the fact that they give many concessions to encourage local industries.

The postal, telegraphic, and telephonic facilities in Bulgaria are quite equal to the average of Europe. There are about 200 post offices, about 7000 miles of telegraph wires, and 600 miles of long-distance telephone. The postal and telegraph administration yields a small surplus to the treasury.

As to the trade of Bulgaria the present is a

difficult time to calculate its value, but before the war the imports were of an annual value of about £4,000,000, and the exports of an annual value of about £4,500,000. The chief import trade is from Austria. England, Turkey, and Germany then follow in that order. The chief markets for Bulgarian exports are Turkey, England, Germany, and Austria. The chief financial institution of the country is the Bulgarian National Bank, which is a State institution, 87 per cent of its profits going to the Bulgarian Government. There are also State savings banks which are much favoured by the thrifty peasantry, there being about 30,000 depositors.

The monetary units which have been adopted by Bulgaria are the *lev* (having the value of one franc) and the *stotinka* (centime), being the hundredth part of a *lev*. For some years after the creation of the Principality, the Government found it impossible to introduce any national coins. It had to permit the circulation of all kinds of foreign money—Servian, Roumanian, Russian, etc. In 1881 the Government put into circulation two million francs of Bulgarian copper money, but these, as well as the twelve millions of silver money which were issued in 1883–84, proved quite insufficient to drive away the foreign money, so that the latter continued to be used in all commercial transactions. It was not until 1887 that the Government prohibited the circulation of Servian and Roumanian coins. Later Russian money was also prohibited, and there is now a purely national currency. On the outbreak of the war in 1913 a *moratorium* was declared, and the internal finance of the country was managed on a paper currency. The confidence of the people kept this paper money at its full value. I was never able to get any concession in exchanging English gold for paper.

Bulgaria, notwithstanding all the preoccupations of a young nation, finds time to encourage the arts. As the illustrations to this volume will show, there is a flourishing school of native art in Bulgaria. To Nicolas Pavlovitch (born 1835, died 1889) belongs the honour of having been the father of modern Bulgarian art. He graduated at the academies in Vienna and Munich, and, after visiting the various museums in Dresden and Prague, exhibited during 1860 in Belgrade two pictures whose subjects had been suggested by ancient Bulgarian history. He then went to Petrograd and Moscow. In 1861 he returned to his native country, where he endeavoured, by means of his lithographs and pictures of subjects both ancient and modern, to stimulate his compatriots to political and intellectual life. He also tried to reform and modernise church painting in accordance with the requirements of modern artistic technique, and made two unsuccessful attempts at opening a school of painting. He painted portraits, and, in the palace of the Pasha of Roustchouk, he illustrated a Turkish history of the Janissaries.

In 1896 a State school of painting was founded at Sofia, and there is now a fine art gallery in the capital. But most of the artistic impulse has come from abroad, and the most notable names in Bulgarian art after that of Pavlovitch are Piotrovsky (Polish), Boloungaro (Italian), de Fourçade (French), Sliapin (Russian). The first art exhibition was organised in 1887 by Ivan Angeloff, teacher in the Gymnasium of Sofia and a graduate of the Munich Academy of Fine Arts. This exhibition, which contained three pictures painted in Bulgaria and a number of sketches and studies dating from the artist's student days in Munich, as well as drawings by students of the Gymnasium, was held in one of the drawing-rooms of the Gymnasium in honour of the Prince, who had recently been elected to the Bulgarian throne. Some five years later, on the occasion of the first Bulgarian Industrial and Agricultural Exhibition, held at Plovdiv in 1892, the first collective art exhibition was organised, the productions of the various Bulgarian artists being exhibited. King Ferdinand is a consistent patron of Bulgarian art, and has the richest collection of pictures in Bulgaria, distributed among his palaces at Sofia, Plovdiv, and Varna.

M. Audrey Protitch, in a recent monograph on Bulgarian art (to which I am indebted for most of the facts above) gives this critical summary of Bulgarian achievement :

If we exclude historical painting, which, since the early and specialised attempts of Nicolas Pavlovitch, has been almost entirely neglected in Bulgaria, Bulgarian artists have tried their hand at almost every form of art. Ethnographical pictures, national scenes, pictures of military subjects, landscapes, interiors, flower pieces, animals, portraits, icons, allegories, mythical subjects, ruins, architecture—all these are fully represented in the art gallery of the National Museum, and have figured in nearly all the art exhibitions. The first place among these varieties is held by landscapes, *genre*, and portraits, whether in oil, water-colour, or pastel. The weak point of Bulgarian artists is undoubtedly undraped figures, especially undraped feminine figures, the only exception being Stephan Ivanoff, who however abandoned this class of work to become the best icon-painter in Bulgaria.

Bulgarian art may be called national only as regards its contents, but neither in form nor technique. As we have already said, the subjects are taken from Bulgarian scenery or from peasant and town life. The sense of human form is gradually developing, with the exception of the feminine body, which remains proscribed by public taste. This last circumstance accounts, to a great extent, for the low level of sculpture in Bulgaria. Decorative art is making rapid strides, owing to the great amount of building going on during recent years. Artistic form and technique are in a transitional phase, all the younger artists waging war against the traditional and conventional styles and the foreign influences that have hitherto hindered the free development of art in Bulgaria, and striving to evolve forms more in conformity with the contents of Bulgarian art.

About Bulgarian literature I can say nothing—lacking a guidance of a competent critic or a knowledge of the language—except that it is ambitious and aspiring. But it can hardly be expected that a language which is, after all, but a dialect of Russian should ever produce a great literature. The Bulgarian national pride is so strong that probably there will never be a movement to make Russian the literary language of the people; but in that would seem to be the best hope of a Bulgarian literature.

CHAPTER XI

HOW BULGARIA IS GOVERNED

To attempt to describe how Bulgaria is governed is to enter inevitably into the realms of controversy. In theory the system of government is purely democratic: and many Bulgarians are confident that the practice follows the theory closely. Personally I have my doubts. The working of a fully democratic constitution seems to be tempered a great deal by the aristocratic powers reserved to the King in Council at times of crisis: and this tempering is probably necessary.

The ancient Bulgarian system of government was without a doubt the despotic tribal system of nomads. Under Turkish rule, the territory of Bulgaria was administered as the Vilayet of the Danube under a Turkish Pasha; and not always badly administered as is proved by the fact that Bulgarian industry and thrift was allowed to raise the province into the most flourishing one of Turkey-in-Europe. But until the Treaty of Paris in 1856, Turkey had no real political organisation. Being a theocratic state, all her public institutions emanated from the Kaliph, as the representative of Mohammed. The Koran took the place of civil and criminal law, and the duty of its ministers was to punish all those who broke its commandments. Every parish had a " cadi," who was appointed by the spiritual chief. The cadi concentrated in his hands all jurisdictions, judging without appeal cases, civil and criminal, and observing no fixed rules of procedure in the application of the few principles which the Koran contained on the subject of civil relations. In certain special cases, the Sheik-ul-Islam of Constantinople, the highest religious tribunal in Turkey, had the right to revise the decisions of the cadis. At the Congress of Paris, Turkey, as one of the participating parties, was admitted into the concert of European Powers. Then civil tribunals were for the first time created in Turkey. In 1867 they were introduced in the Vilayet of the Danube by the then Governor-General, Midhat Pasha. In 1877 the Russians liberated Bulgaria from the Turks. After the Treaty of Berlin

A GRAVE QUESTION

Prince Dondoukoff-Korsakoff framed a provisional system of government for Bulgaria. Then a Russian law professor, Gradovsky, with the help of General Domontovity, framed a constitution for Bulgaria. This was based upon the commune being, as in Russia, the organic unit of administrative control, and was aristocratic rather than democratic in its general character, though it provided for a far more liberal system of government than that existing in Russia herself.

The draft Constitution was submitted to a Constituent Assembly elected by the Bulgarian people at Tirnova in February 1879. The Assembly elected a Committee of fifteen members to consider the draft. This Committee revised the draft, making it less democratic than before. The Assembly rejected their revision and set to work to recast the Constitution, making it far more liberal, and including a provision for universal suffrage. The Constitution thus revised was affirmed and has been in force since, with occasional suspensions when the Prince for a time took autocratic power. Since 1883 the Constitution has not been suspended.

The main principles of the Bulgarian Constitution are :

(1) Separation of public authorities into legislative, executive and judiciary.

(2) Equality of citizens, as regards civil and political rights.

(3) Inviolability of the person, residence, property, and correspondence.

(4) Liberty of conscience, liberty of the press, liberty of public meetings, and liberty to form associations.

(5) Direct and secret universal suffrage for the election of members of the National Assembly, and departmental and municipal councils.

(6) Local self-government.

The authorities under the constitution are:

1. The king, who is head of the army and navy, has the supreme executive power and can appoint and dismiss ministers, can prorogue Parliament but not for longer than two months, and can dissolve Parliament. The King may issue regulations and order measures, having the obligatory force of laws, whenever the State is threatened with immediate internal or external danger. All such measures, however, must be adopted by the Cabinet Council, and entail the collective responsibility of all the ministers. They must be submitted to the approval of the

National Assembly in the course of its earliest session. A special section of the Constitution expressly forbids the levying, by means of such extraordinary regulations, of new taxes or duties, the National Assembly having alone the right to impose them.

2. The National Assembly, elected by manhood suffrage through a secret ballot. Every deputy has the right to make propositions and to introduce bills, if he is supported by one-fourth of the members present. The National Assembly may amend the bills and propositions introduced by the Government. The deputies have the right to make interpellations. By means of this, the deputies can force individual ministers or the entire Government to explain their line of conduct and to state their intentions on some special matter, or as regards their general policy. The National Assembly may appoint commissions of inquiry or institute inquiries as regards the conduct of the Government. It may submit to the Crown special addresses.

There is no Upper House, but for special occasions a " Grand National Assembly " is convoked. This has the same composition as the ordinary National Assembly, and its members are elected in the same way. The only difference between the two is that the number of members of a Grand National Assembly is twice that of the ordinary National Assembly, every electoral unit of 20,000 inhabitants sending two deputies instead of one. The Grand National Assembly may decide only those matters which have necessitated its convocation. A Grand National Assembly is called in the following cases :

1. To decide questions of exchanging or ceding a portion of the territory of Bulgaria.

2. To revise the Constitution.

3. To elect a new Prince when the reigning family becomes extinct, owing to absence of descendants who can occupy the throne.

4. To appoint regents during the minority of the heir to the throne.

5. To authorise the Prince to accept the government of another State.

Every Order must bear, in addition to the signature of the Prince, that of one minister or of all the ministers, these latter being the responsible representatives of the executive authority. The ministers are held responsible to the Prince and to the National Assembly for all their acts. This responsibility is collective for all the ministers in the case of measures which have been decided by the Council of Ministers, and individual with respect to the acts of the ministers as heads of the various State Departments.

What I have described represents in effect a complete system of representative and responsible government. But observation of Bulgarian politics during and since the war has suggested to me that the King and his ministers really can exercise a practical oligarchy: and it is probably necessary that they should.

In the Bulgarian National Assembly there is a very strong Socialist party, and the Parliamentary life of the Kingdom is stormy.

CHAPTER XII

THE FUTURE OF BULGARIA

It is impossible, in my opinion, to doubt the future of Bulgaria. The disasters of 1914 would seem to suggest that the Bulgarian nation was without the moral balance to withstand the intoxication of victory. But whilst the events of that unhappy year showed the lack of that balance, the fault was with the leaders of the people rather than with the people themselves.

The misfortune of Bulgaria in this generation of the nation's life—a misfortune which is being rapidly repaired—is that she has no middle class : and no class with any " tradition " of leadership behind it. There are the peasants—admirable material for nation-making—heroic, thrifty, moral, industrious, practical. Above the peasants there is no class from which to draw a good supply of competent administrators, law-makers, officers, professional men. The peasant has his own limited capacities for leadership; but they are limited. I have encountered him frequently as Mayor of some little commune, as captain of an infantry regiment, and admired his administrative abilities, within a narrow and familiar scope, exceedingly. But the peasant does not go higher than that. It is the son of the peasant with some extra gift of cleverness who is "given an education," who becomes legislator, official, cleric, diplomat. In many cases he does not take his polish well. Advanced education for the ambitious Balkan lad has in the past generally meant education abroad; and in Paris or Vienna or Petrograd the young Bulgarian, plunged into an altogether new life of luxury and of frivolity, often suffered a loss of natural strength of fibre for which no book-learning could compensate.

That evil will pass away. It is now possible to get a fairly advanced liberal education without going beyond Bulgaria. Also the people are becoming more immune to the effects of Western civilisation. Measles is a dangerous, indeed generally fatal, disease in countries to which it is first introduced. But in time immunity comes to make it almost harmless. Bulgaria's material for a modern national organisation is being quickly improved by the upgrowth of a middle class whose sons will be able to keep their Bulgarian qualities even under the circumstances of life in Paris or other great modern city. In future, then, the courage of the people is likely to have a wiser, more reasonable leadership, and, with that, it will do wonders.

But I do not wish to be misunderstood as representing that to-day the official classes and the leaders of the Bulgarian nation are generally unworthy or incompetent. That would be very far from the truth. But it is the truth that as yet Bulgaria has not a class sufficient in numbers and strong enough in tradition to supply her needs in leadership. How could it be otherwise, seeing that the nation is not much more than a generation old, and has had to begin working up its organisation from bed-rock?

The events of 1913–14 have left Bulgaria weak in her greatest element of national strength —in the numbers of her citizens. The wars with the Turks and the subsequent war with the other Balkan states, the ravages of cholera and, one may unhappily conclude too, the ravages

A YOUNG MAN OF THE CHOUMLA DISTRICT

THE FUTURE OF BULGARIA 177

of hunger after the dreadful ordeals of the successive campaigns, have taken heavy toll of Bulgarian manhood. But the country will " stock up " quickly. Its birth-rate is the highest in the world ; and its " effective " birth-rate, *i.e.* the proportion of survivals of those born, is also the highest. If only a period of peace can be secured, all will be well in time.

Poor as were her acquisitions of territory compared with her hopes from the war, Bulgaria at least won a free outlet to the open sea. Her ports on the Black Sea were always felt to be of limited use, because traffic to and from them had to pass through the Dardanelles and was therefore at the mercy of Turkey in case of war. But now Bulgaria has free access to the Aegean Sea, and though without a good port has a possible port there.

Considerations of strategic position and of territorial acquisition are, however, of minor importance in considering Bulgaria's future. It is in the character of the Bulgarian race and the conditions of life encouraging the growth of that sturdy character in which the hopes of that future are bound up. The young Bulgarian is born usually in the country, and usually also as one of a large family. Here is an interesting table—compiled before the war—showing at once the proportion of urban and rural population and the prevalence of large families in Bulgaria:

Number of Members of Families.	Number of such Families.		Number of Members of Families.	Number of such Families.	
	In Towns.	In the Country.		In Towns.	In the Country.
1	19,299	11,807	11	737	11,506
2	22,311	25,035	12	340	7,570
3	28,182	45,747	13	180	4,853
4	29,732	66,554	14	79	3,446
5	27,884	82,771	15	44	2,187
6	21,746	83,635	16	39	1,499
7	13,636	69,216	17	16	1,069
8	7,619	48,218	18	14	786
9	3,646	30,756	19	8	528
10	1,757	19,005	20	1	368

The Bulgarian infant in the beginning of life will have no handicap of artificial feeding. The " feeding bottle " is practically unknown in his country. From the very early age of three this Bulgarian infant may begin to go to school. Primary education is obligatory. The infant schools are for the preparation of the children for the primary schools. Infants between the ages of three and five years are admitted in the lower divisions, and those between five and six in the higher division. They are taught games, songs, drawing, manual work, and simple arithmetic. The teaching in these schools is entrusted exclusively to school mistresses.

The proclaimed object of the primary school is "to give the future citizen a moral education, to develop him physically, and to give him the most indispensable knowledge." The studies last four years. The school year begins on September 1 and lasts, in the towns, until June 25, and in the villages until the beginning of May. Thus the whole summer and part of the autumn is exempt from school duties—a wise exemption in an agricultural community where the children, and perhaps some of the teachers, have to work in the fields. The subjects taught include morals, catechism, Bulgarian and ancient Bulgarian history, civic instruction, geography, arithmetic, natural history, drawing, singing, gymnastics, manual work (for boys), and embroidery (for girls). Every parish or village of more than fifty houses must have at least one primary school. The hamlets and villages of less than fifty houses are considered, for educational purposes, as parishes.

The enactment rendering public instruction

obligatory extends to all children between the ages of six and twelve. The only temporary or permanent exception allowed by the law is in favour of children physically or intellectually unfit. Disobedience to the law is punished by fines.

Ordinary education ceases with the primary schools or with the private schools for Mohammedans and Jews which the Bulgarian law allows to be maintained. The cost to the State of the education of each child at these schools is less than £1 a year, of which the State provides rather more than half, the communes the other half.

Thus the young Bulgarian gets a fairly sound start in life, so far as schooling is concerned, if he intends to go on the land or to follow an industrial occupation. If he, or she, has greater ambitions, there are gymnasia for boys and high schools for girls. At these gymnasia the subjects of instruction are religious knowledge, Bulgarian, French, German, Russian, Latin and Greek languages, history, geography and civic instruction, arithmetic, geometry and geometrical drawing, algebra, descriptive geometry, physics, chemistry, natural science, psychology, logic and ethics, and gymnastics. The subjects of instruction at the girls' high schools include most of those mentioned above and also hygiene and the rearing of children, domestic economy, embroidery, music and singing. There are further special pedagogical schools for the training of teachers, and there is a University at Sofia having chairs for Historico-Philological, Physico-Mathematical, and legal courses. This University is beginning to take the place of foreign universities for the training of young Bulgaria for public life. The training is narrower but, on the whole, probably better from a national point of view. Only the more seasoned minds of a young nation should be submitted to the test of foreign study.

But let us get back to the young Bulgarian who is going on the land. At the age of twelve he leaves school and henceforth devotes himself wholly, instead of partly, to work on his father's farm. He begins, too, to be introduced to the work of the village commune, though he may not take any part in its control for some time yet. With great care the makers of the Bulgarian Constitution have tried to guarantee the independence of the communes. The central government must take no part in the administration of the communes, nor maintain any agents of its own to interfere with their affairs. The commune, which forms the basis of the State fabric, enjoys thus a complete autonomy. It is the smallest unit in the administrative organisation of the country. Every district is subdivided into communes, which are either urban or rural. Every Bulgarian subject must belong to a commune and figure in its registers, or else he is a vagrant and punishable as such. The commune is governed by a Mayor and Council, and at the age of twenty-five the Bulgarian is eligible to become a councillor. Not only is the commune the organ of local government, but it has much to do with the control of the land affairs of this nation of peasant proprietors.

At nineteen the Bulgarian youth, at seventeen the Bulgarian girl are marriageable, and their parents set about the work of mating them as quickly as possible. Marriages are almost always arranged by the parents, and it is not usual for husband and wife to come from different communes. After marriage the Bulgarian wife is supposed to devote herself exclusively to family life and not to wish for any social life.

There is an almost *harem* system of seclusion, but — except that the Bulgarian is monogamous in theory and generally in practice, whilst the Turk is polygamous in theory and usually monogamous by force of circumstances, since he cannot afford more than one wife—the Bulgarian idea of home life shows evidence of Turkish influences.

The Bulgarian civil law gives to the Church complete control of the matters of marriage and divorce. Divorce is allowed on various grounds, but is not common. Adultery does not of itself entail the dissolution of marriage. The party which has been found guilty of adultery is not allowed to marry the partner in guilt. The custody of the children, in case of divorce, is given to the innocent party, except when the children are below the age of five years, in which case they are left with the mother. Mutual consent of the married is not a ground for divorce. All marriages contracted in opposition to the canon laws are considered null. The Diocesan Council is the sole competent authority to judge affairs of divorce, its decisions being submitted to the approval of a metropolitan bishop.

I think Gibbon was responsible in the first

instance for ascribing to the Bulgarians a low moral character. But all the evidence that came under my notice suggested that the Bulgarians were exceptionally virtuous.

In their hospitals I found no cases of disease arising from vice. In their camps they had no women followers. I passed through many villages which their troops had traversed, and never observed any evidence of women having been interfered with.

The young Bulgarian, married—without much romance in the wooing, but perhaps none the less happily married for that according to his ideas—tilling his little farm, joins now in the main current of the national life. He is exceedingly industrious, rising early and working late. His food is frugal — whole - meal bread, hard cheese, soft cheese (which is like rank butter), vegetables, very occasionally meat and eggs. From his Turk cousins he has acquired a love of sweetmeats, and so for his treats lollies and cakes are essential. But also he is a Slav and likes a glass of *vodka* on Sundays and feast days. He is very sober, however, and drunkenness is rare. His chief drink is water, with now and again tea made in the Russian fashion, or coffee

A BULGARIAN FARM

THE FUTURE OF BULGARIA

made in the Turkish fashion. At the village *cafés* these are the chief refreshments — *vodka*, tea and coffee. But a light beer is also brewed in Bulgaria, and drunk by the inhabitants.

Both as regards food and drink, however, the Bulgarians' habits are usually governed by an intense frugality. The country gives no very rich return to the peasant. He almost invariably marries young and has a large family. The household budget thus leaves very little margin over from the strictly necessary food-expenses. That margin the Bulgarian prefers in the main to save rather than to dissipate. The Bulgarian is economical, not to say grasping. He dreams always of getting a little richer. In his combination of the instincts of a cultivator and of a trader he resembles a great deal the French Norman peasantry.

The duties of national defence make heavy demands on the national industry in Bulgaria. Training for military service is universal and compulsory. There is no hope at all that there will be any lightening of military burdens for some time to come, since the 1914 wars have left Bulgaria in a position which the national pride refuses to accept as final. The burdens are borne cheerfully. The patience of the Bulgarian peasant soldiery during the awful campaigns of 1913 and 1914 was heroic, and their steadiness in the field showed how well they had profited by their training.

For this Bulgarian nation, so frugal, industrious, persevering and courageous there must be a splendid future. It has all the essential elements of greatness and must overcome in time the misfortunes of the past. If but the Fates will shield Bulgaria for a time from the desperate policy of attempting any new war of revenge or of enterprise, her growing economic strength, her superiority in industry and in application to other peoples of the Peninsula will in time assert themselves, and give her a strong position in the Balkans.

CHAPTER XIII

THE RESPONSIBILITY OF EUROPE

As this book goes to the press there is again war in the Balkans. It is only a little war certainly, as yet confined within the limits of the " autonomous State " of Albania, that quaint creation of the ambitions of Austria and Italy, which in its foundation suggested the custom of one of the old Fiji cannibal tribes—that of keeping alive and fattening a victim whom it was intended to eat. Austria desires the Adriatic shore of the Balkan Peninsula : so does Italy. They cannot agree either to fight out the issue now or to abandon their conflicting ambitions ; and they have been responsible for creating " independent Albania," which one of them hopes to devour up in the near future when the other one is in difficulties. This war, small as it now is, threatens, however, to spread to a great one; and though the danger may pass away now for the moment, it is certain that one near day Albania will be the cause of another Balkan war: for it is to kindle that war that she has been brought into existence. Even to-day the position is immediately threatening. The creation of Albania gave to Montenegro, to Servia, and to Greece a serious disappointment. In particular was it a blow to Montenegro, whose heroic little people had through centuries borne the chief brunt of the fighting against the Turk:

> They rose to where their sovran eagle sails,
> They kept their faith, their freedom, on the height,
> Chaste, frugal, savage, arm'd by day and night
> Against the Turk; whose inroad nowhere scales
> Their headlong passes, but his footstep fails,
> And red with blood the Crescent reels from fight
> Before their dauntless hundreds, in prone flight
> By thousands down the crags and thro' the vales.
> O smallest among peoples! rough rock-throne
> Of Freedom! warriors beating back the swarm
> Of Turkish Islam for five hundred years,
> Great Tsernogora! never since thine own
> Black ridges drew the cloud and brake the storm
> Has breathed a race of mightier mountaineers.[1]

By the creation of Albania Montenegro was debarred from any great territorial gain out of the partition of the Turks' old estate in the

---

[1] Tennyson's well-known sonnet.

THE RESPONSIBILITY OF EUROPE 189

Balkans, and was shut back on her mountains, as it seemed irrevocably. Servia and Greece were left with almost as serious grievances. Albania therefore is a constant source of temptation to a war of enterprise on the part of three of the Balkan nations, and the war only awaits a favourable opportunity to break out : a pretext for it can always be supplied at a day's notice by some border collision with the wild and lawless Albanian clans. Should the war in Albania spread to her neighbours, Bulgaria, outraged and mortified by the Treaty of Bucharest and again robbed and humiliated by Turkish encroachments on her powerlessness after that Treaty, in all probability will seize the opportunity to make a war of requital on some one of her neighbours, and the Balkan Peninsula will then be again drenched in blood. There will be again a cry of shocked horror from Western Europe as to these " quarrelsome and bloodthirsty " Balkan peoples. But in fair play and justice there is more reason for the little Balkan peoples to be shocked and horrified at the cold-blooded policy of the Great Powers who, for their own ends, create conditions which make peace in the Balkans impossible.

The truth is that these little shreds of peoples, in the blood-soaked Peninsula which destiny marked out to be the great battle-ground of races, have been used as pawns in the great game of European diplomacy ever since the fall of Napoleon. It will be recalled that one of the earlier dreams of that ambitious genius was to enter the service of the Sublime Porte and re-organise the power of Turkey. The crumbling away of the power of the Turkish Empire, which had given centuries of anxiety to Christian Europe, was at that time apparent. A great genius might then have restored the fighting power and the prestige of Islam. But Napoleon turned to other work and Turkey went on decaying. There soon arose a question as to who should be the legatee of the "Sick Man of Europe," and legacy hunters, some fawning, some clamorous, gathered at his bedside. To some of these it soon occurred that there would be wisdom in hastening the process of division, and that a means to do this was to question the moral right of the Turk to the Christian provinces over which he ruled. In the state of public feeling in Europe at the time it was most convenient to question this right on the ground of the religious intolerance of the Turk.

Without joining the party of the " pro-Turks " it is clear that that ground was more of a pretext than a reality. The Turk is not a religious persecutor to anything like the extent to which the Christian has been a religious persecutor. On coming into Europe he never sought, for example, to destroy the Greek Church, and I do not think that there is any clear evidence that Turkish misrule was founded at any period on intolerance carried to the degree of murder for faith's sake. The fault rather of the Porte's rule was the dreadful corruption and incompetence of the Turk as an administrator and the Turkish ideas of the status of women-folk—ideas which gave to Moslem women rights derived from their Moslem men-relatives, but regarded Christian women as if they were cattle without owners. I think that it was the adoption by European Powers of religion as a pretext for interfering in the Balkans which has been largely responsible for the religious bitterness there. It would make the situation more clear and give a better hope for the future if Western Europe would frankly recognise that the fervid interest taken in the Balkan Peninsula for about a century has had no other reason generally than territory-hunger.

When Turkey began showing signs of falling to pieces, Russia made an early claim to the succession of " the Sick Man's " estate. Russia wanted a warm water-port; and her territories would have been nicely rounded off by the acquisition of Turkey in Europe. These were the real reasons, not publicly expressed, for her Balkan policy. Less real reasons, kept in the foreground, were that the head of the Russian Orthodox Church was at Constantinople, that Russia was the kinsman of the Slav populations in the Balkans, and that her duty and right was to liberate co-religionists who were suffering from religious persecution.

Great Britain was the great obstacle to the desire of Russia to march down upon Constantinople. Her real objection was that with Russia on the Bosphorus the control of the Mediterranean might pass into the hands of the rival who seemed to wish to dispute with her for the mastery of India. Her expressed reasons had some vague declarations about the " chivalry of the Turk." Austria developed her ambition

A YOUNG WOMAN OF THE ROUSTCHOUK DISTRICT

THE RESPONSIBILITY OF EUROPE

to suzerainty over the Balkan Peninsula mainly on the strength of a claim to be the heir of the old Holy Roman Empire, and as such possessing an hereditary right to rule over the old seat of that Empire in the East. Italy was forced into a Balkan policy by the impossibility of allowing a rival Power to settle on the other side of the Adriatic, threatening her whole east coast. Germany and France came into Balkan politics chiefly as allies of Powers with more direct interests, although both have now fears and hopes regarding the Asiatic dominions of the Sublime Porte and shape their Balkan policy accordingly.

The way in which, by the Congress of Berlin, the Treaty of San Stefano was changed illustrated well the fact that, as regards the Balkan Peninsula, Europe was far more concerned to advance the ambitions of the Western Powers than to ameliorate the condition of the Near Eastern peoples under Turkish government. The other Powers' jealousy of Russia vetoed the creation of the big Bulgaria suggested then, because it was feared that Bulgarian gratitude to the Power which had been responsible for her liberation would make the new kingdom a mere appanage of Russia. When it was manifest afterwards that Bulgarian gratitude was not of that high and disinterested quality, and that the young Bulgarian nation was, though semi-Eastern in origin, sufficiently European to play for her own hand, and her own hand only, in national affairs, Europe had a spasm of remorse and approved when Bulgaria took advantage of a Turkish misfortune to gather to herself Eastern Roumelia. The only Power that objected to that acquisition was Russia. Her eagerness for a big Bulgaria had faded away with the knowledge that Bulgaria, big or little, was not inclined to submit to dictation in national affairs from Russia.

The position after the Treaty of Berlin in the Balkans was this: four virtually independent small nations held old Turkish provinces, and each desired eagerly, and claimed on historical grounds, extensions of their territory at the expense of the Turk or at the expense of one another. Each was tempted to try the means to its end of intrigue with one of the great Powers. These Powers, still keeping in view their own ambitions, looked upon and treated the Balkan States as instruments to be used or to be discarded without reference to the happiness of

THE RESPONSIBILITY OF EUROPE 195

the Balkans and with sole reference to the "European situation." Put a group of hungry and badly trained boys in a cake-shop; set over them as a Board of Appeal unjust, selfish, and intriguing masters; and you may not expect peace. That has been for nearly a century the position in the Balkans.

The Balkan League between Bulgaria, Servia, Greece, and Montenegro, formed about 1912, offered the first steady hope of a peaceful settlement in the peninsula. There was the beginning there of a movement which might have developed on the lines of the Swiss Federation and grown to a Balkan Power in which the Slav element and the Graeco-Roman element could have combined, in spite of differences of language and of religion. The fact that Roumania stood out of the League was the first unfavourable circumstance. True, Roumania is not a Balkan State in the strict sense of the word, but her national destiny is clearly to be either a partner with the Balkan States or the humble friend of one of the great Powers on her borders. This fact is recognised now, and for the time being Roumania is actually the head of a loose Balkan combination formed in 1913.

More dangerous to the future of the Balkan League than the abstention of Roumania was the fact that it had to face the strong hostility of Austria, and therefore of the Triple Alliance; and it had hardly the warm sympathy of Russia and was not therefore strongly favoured by the Triple Entente. Great Britain, whose interests were all to be served and not hindered by the growth of a Balkan Power, was the only strong friend the Balkan League had; and her friendship was not strong enough to make her support a matter of definite national policy.

If Europe had had an unselfish interest in the Balkans it would have welcomed the Balkan League and made every effort to consolidate its unity. True, the Balkan League had as its first task the robbing of Turkey of her European provinces. But Turkey was herself in the position of a robber; and it had come to be a matter of practical agreement among the European Powers that the Christian provinces of Turkey would soon have to pass from under the rule of the Sublime Porte. The only question left was " how ? " The Balkan League offered to answer that question in a way satisfactory to all unselfish interests. But the selfish interests of Europe

THE RESPONSIBILITY OF EUROPE

were not served by the League. Austria, dreaming of one day marching down to the Aegean, saw that that hope would be shattered if a strong Balkan Federation held the Balkan Peninsula. Italy was afraid of another Power on the Adriatic—an unwise fear, because her true national policy should have welcomed a new check to Austria. Russia was not eager to welcome a Balkan Federation, in which possibly the Slav element would not predominate and which, in any case, would get to Constantinople inevitably in the course of events. A bevy of eager jealousies set to work to put obstacles in the path of the Balkan League. Those Powers which were friendly to it were mildly friendly; those which were hostile were relentlessly hostile.

It would be perhaps too much to say that if the European Powers had been benevolently neutral to the Balkan League it would have survived and set firm the foundations of a Balkan Federation. But it is reasonable to believe that an actively benevolent Europe, acting with firmness and impartiality and without seeking to serve any selfish aims, would have succeeded in keeping the League together and saving the series of fratricidal wars which began in 1913 and will be continued as soon as the present exhaustion has been relieved. Instead of an actively benevolent there was an actively malevolent Europe.

The plans of the Balkan League contemplated a division of the territory which is now Albania between Greece, Servia, and Montenegro. The decree of the Powers, issued because Austria made a "bluffing threat" of war if Servia were allowed territory on the Adriatic, was that Albania should be an independent kingdom. It had at the time no cities, no railways, no roads worthy of the name, no civilised organisation, no basis at all of national life. Several different racial types and religions found a shelter within its area. The only useful purpose that could be served by creating Albania as an independent State was to give the Balkan League a cause of disunion, and to provide a *pied-à-terre* for Austria for future operations in the Balkans. If the "Holy Roman Empire" had abandoned all thought of getting to the Aegean there would have been no Albania.

The Balkan League was already very shaky when this bone of contention was thrown among its members. Servia, Montenegro, and Greece, now deprived of a share of their spoil, sought to obtain from Bulgaria, who was in the position, as it were, of residuary legatee, some concessions out of her share. Bulgaria, embittered at the time by the fact that Roumania had taken advantage of the situation to demand a territorial grant south of the Danube, was unwisely obstinate and would make no concession to any of her partners. The issue had to be fought out through a disastrous war in which Bulgaria, Servia, and Greece were bled further of their manhood, already sadly thinned in the war with Turkey.

The Albania which was the chief of the causes of that fratricidal war was duly constituted, and Prince William of Wied appointed Mpret or King. At once there was trouble on all the Albanian boundaries, but chiefly in the south, where the province of Epirus wished to be Greek and rose in revolt against the new Albanian Government. The effect of that revolt, which was generally successful, was that the Epirus district seems likely to win a measure of local government or Home Rule founded on the following chief conditions :

The country is divided into two administrative districts known as Koritza and Argyrocastro. These will be governed by two Prefects nominated by the Albanian Government. In all local councils the number of elected members is to be three in excess of the *ex officio* members.

All existing Greek religious institutions and privileges are to remain unaltered.

The Greek language is to be taught in the three first classes of the popular schools, together with the Albanian language. In the schools of purely Greek communities only the Greek language will be taught.

The Greek language is to be recognised in matters of local administration and the Law Courts in the two districts.

The native Epirotes are to remain armed, and are to be incorporated in the *gendarmerie* commanded by Dutch officers. All other volunteers are to leave the country.

Albania is to grant a full amnesty.

The new regime is to be organised and its execution controlled by the International Commission, and the Commissioners are to visit the country to see that its provisions are being given effect to.

Thus already it is recognised that within the small territory of Albania there has been included one district which is so Greek in sympathy that it cannot be administered under Albanian law.

The next development in Albania was that Essad Pasha, the Albanian chief who had, more than any other, assisted to form an independent Albania, fell out with Prince William and was arrested. A state of tension between him and

AT THE WELL

THE RESPONSIBILITY OF EUROPE 201

Prince William had increased as evidence of Essad Pasha's complicity in a revolutionary movement became known. A letter written by Essad Pasha fell into Prince William's hands, in which Essad Pasha ordered his agents to persuade people to obey only his commands and not those of the Prince. The Prince thereupon summoned him to the Palace, and after a stormy scene Essad Pasha tendered his resignation and returned home. The Prince then held a Council with his Dutch officers, and decided to compel the disbandment of Essad Pasha's bodyguard. A Dutch officer conveyed the Prince's command to Essad Pasha. He at first appeared to consent, and then told his men to resist. They began to fire upon the Prince's armed adherents in the street. Austrian and Italian detachments landed, and a party under the command of an Italian officer arrested Essad Pasha.

That arrest created fresh trouble, and a few days later Prince William abandoned his kingdom and took refuge on a foreign warship. Repenting of that precipitate step, he returned to his capital again, and at the time of writing (June 1914) he is still there under the protection of his foreign soldiers; but an insurgent force holds the field, demanding "restoration of Moslem rule." It is not too much to say that independent Albania has been still-born. Probably neither Austria nor Italy expected such a quick collapse of their artificial creation. But that it would collapse one day must have been within their knowledge and their desire, which was to put a sick infant in the place of a sick man. As it happens, the collapse has come when neither of them is in a position to benefit immediately by it. Neither is prepared for an expedition to the Balkans. But whilst not serving the interests of the Powers who created Albania, this new development has set the Balkan pot seething again. A smell of blood taints the air and general fighting may follow. Albania has provided the latest example of how the selfish ambition of Western European Powers can inflict woe upon the Near East.

Agreed that these peoples of the Near East are very cantankerous and very prone by nature to fly at one another's throats, still I maintain that if Western Europe ceased from interference there would be a better chance of peace in the Balkans, and if she interfered benevolently and unselfishly she could make the certainty of peace.

THE RESPONSIBILITY OF EUROPE

If one could imagine the Powers of Europe reformed as regards their foreign policy, and genuinely anxious to smooth away the troubles of these sorely vexed Balkan peoples, the chief danger left to tranquillity would be the religious intolerance which grows so rankly in the Peninsula —between Christian and Christian more than between Moslem and Christian. There needs to be put up in church or mosque of every Balkan village the inscription of Abul Fazl :

O God, in every temple I see people that see Thee, and in every language I hear spoken, people praise Thee.

Polytheism and Islâm feel after Thee.

Each religion says, " Thou art one, without equal."

If it be a mosque, people murmur the holy prayer, and if it be a Christian church, people ring the bell from love to Thee.

Sometimes I frequent the Christian cloister, and sometimes the mosque.

But it is Thee whom I search from temple to temple.

Thy elect have no dealings with either heresy or orthodoxy; for neither of them stands behind the screen of Thy truth.

Heresy to the heretic, and religion to the orthodox.

But the dust of the rose-petal belongs to the heart of the perfume-seller.

Or the English poet's rendering of it :

                    Shall the rose
Cry to the lotus " No flower thou " ? the palm
Call to the cypress " I alone am fair " ?
The mango spurn the melon at his foot ?

"Mine is the one fruit Alla made for man."
Look how the living pulse of Alla beats
Thro' all His world. If every single star
Should shriek its claim "I only am in heaven,"
Why that were such sphere-music as the Greek
Had hardly dream'd of. There is light in all,
And light, with more or less of shade, in all
Man-modes of worship.   .   .   .   .   .

I hate the rancour of their castes and creeds,
I let men worship as they will, I reap
No revenue from the field of unbelief.
I cull from every faith and race the best
And bravest soul for counsellor and friend.
I loathe the very name of infidel.
I stagger at the Korân and the sword.
I shudder at the Christian and the stake.

In regard also to this tendency to religious strife the older civilisations of Europe could give help if they would, rather than hindrance as they do now, encouraging and stimulating creed jealousies. Even well-meaning and unselfish friends of the Balkans contribute often to spread evil tendencies because they take up the attitude of blind partisanship for one particular Balkan people, and refuse either to give charity to the others or chiding to their pet people.

It would be neither truthful nor good policy to attempt to maintain that the great Powers of Europe are altogether responsible for the blood torrents which are always flowing in the Balkans. But they have had a great share of the responsibility in the past; are very guilty in the present. Since gaining some knowledge of the Balkan peoples I have always nursed a hope, a very desperate hope, that the powers of Western Europe would repent of selfish ambitions at the eleventh hour, and would adopt a policy of real help to the struggling nationalities of the Near East. They are kept so miserable and yet naturally are really so amiable, those little peoples. The Bulgarians in particular I learned to regard with something of affection. Their good temper and their industry and their patience recalled Tolstoy's pen-pictures of the Russian peasants:

All of these peasants, even those who had quarrelled with him about the hay, or those whom he had injured if their intention was not to cheat him, saluted him gaily as they passed, and showed no anger for what he had done, or any remorse or even remembrance that they had tried to defraud him. All was swallowed up and forgotten in this sea of joyous, universal labour. God gave the day, God gave the strength; and the day and the strength consecrated the labour and yielded their own reward. No one dreamed of asking, Why this work, and who enjoyed the fruits of it? These questions were secondary and of no account. . . .

Levin had often looked with interest at this life, had

often been tempted to become one with the people, living their lives; but to-day the impression of what he had seen in the bearing of Vanka Parmenof towards his young wife gave him for the first time a clear and definite desire to exchange the burdensome, idle, artificial, selfish existence which he led, for the laborious, simple, pure, and delightful life of the peasantry.

The elder, who had been sitting with him, had already gone home; the neighbouring villagers were wending their way indoors; while those who lived at a distance were preparing to spend the night in the meadow, and getting ready for supper.

Levin, without being seen, still lay on the hay, looking, listening, and thinking. The peasantry, gathered on the prairie, scarcely slept throughout the short summer night. At first there were gay gossip and laughter while everybody was eating; then followed songs and jests.

All the long, laborious day had left no trace upon them, except of its happiness. . . .

The Bulgarian peasants are indeed very close to the Russians of the south, where there has been a mixture of Tartar blood. Simple, laborious, religious, frugal, they deserve better than to be food for powder.

INDEX

Adrianople, 88
Aegean Sea, 16, 151
Albania, 134
Arjenli, 114

Balkan Mountains, 150
Baltic shores, the, 16
Banki, 153
Black Sea, 16, 150
Bourgas, 20, 161
Bulair, 136
Burgas, 150

Chatalja, 114

Danube, 39
Dardanelles, 145

Epirus, 134
Ermenikioi, 114

Gabrovo, 155

Hissar, 153

Jambouli, 20
Janina, 134

Kalofer, 155
Karlovo, 155
Kasilagatch, 67
Kastoria, 67
Kirk Kilisse, 67, 111

Klissoura, 155
Koprivchtitza, 155
Kotel, 155
Kustendji, 16

Macedonia, 134, 145
Maritza River, 148
Marmora, Sea of, 19, 145
Meritchléri, 153
Monastir, 67
Mustapha Pasha, 67, 108

Nisch, 67
Nish in Servia, near the border of Bulgaria, 21
Novo-grad, 18

Panaguiourichté, 155
Philippopolis, 18, 67, 154
Pirdop, 155
Preslav—now in ruins, 54

Rhodope Mountains, 59, 150
Roumania, 150
Roustchouk, 67

Salonica, 145
Samokov, 155
Sandjaks, 67
Schumla, 18, 33
Scutari, 134
Servia, 150
Shipka Pass, 96,

INDEX

Silistra, 150
Silivri, 114
Sliven, 67, 153, 155
Sofia, 22, 67, 77, 153
Sopot, 155
Stara Zagora, 106, 154
Stroumitza, 67
Struma River, 151

Tchorlu, 113
Thrace, 33, 134, 145

Tikvesch, 67
Tirnova, 67, 169
Toultcha, 67
Trevna, 155

Uskub, 67

Varna, 16, 67, 150, 161
Varshetz, 153
Velès, 67
Vidin, 67

THE END

Printed by R. & R. CLARK, LIMITED, *Edinburgh*.

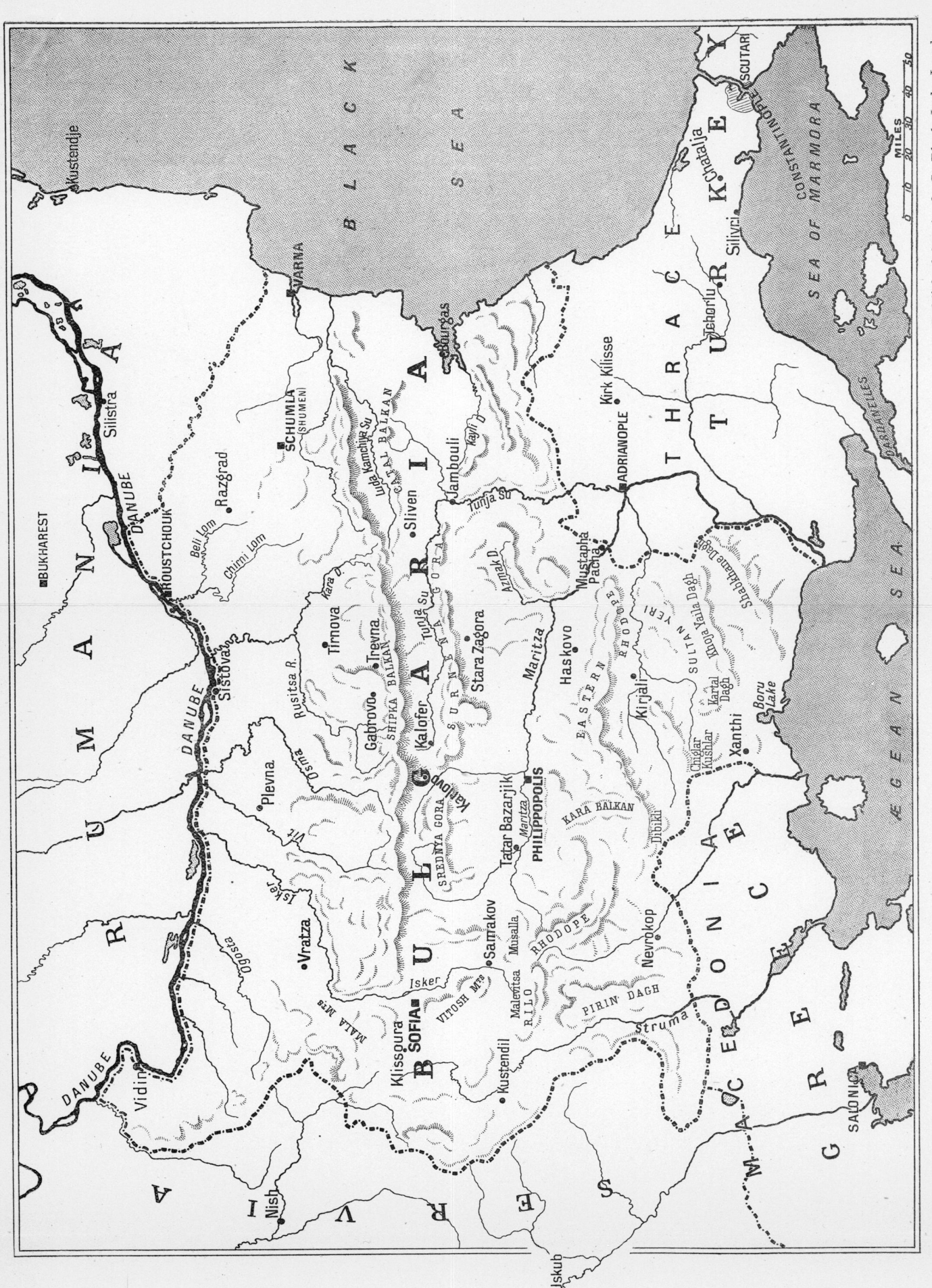

Sketch Map accompanying "Bulgaria." By Frank Fox.